The
Broken
Vase

ADVANCED PRAISE FOR BROKEN VASE

"This book is very personal and very real. It brings us close to the experience of losing a child, and all of the heartbreak that entails. It is also a book of grappling with faith and finding hope in the midst of darkness–an important book for anyone who has lost a child or knows someone who has."

—Sherri Mandell, author of
"The Blessing of a Broken Heart"
and Director of the Koby Mandell Foundation

"No greater love, no greater loss, no greater challenge: A mother's journey from despair to transcendence, harrowingly experienced, beautifully told."

—Tova Reich, author, most recently of
"The House of Love and Prayer and Other Stories"

"In her heart wrenching and deeply personal book, "The Broken Vase," Yaffa Klugerman powerfully and poignantly describes the shattering pain that those of us who have lost children on the roads experience and the courageous steps we must take to rebuild even as we remember. Yaffa's journey is one of courage, resilience and inspiration. Her words offer solace, strength, and a reminder that even in our deepest sorrow, hope and healing are possible."

—Rochelle Sobel, President,
Association for Safe International Road Travel

ADVANCED PRAISE FOR BROKEN VASE

"Memoirs of a child's death are often a recounting of facts, a litany that must be verified on the page for the parent author to believe their impossible truth. In "The Broken Vase," Yaffa Klugerman's exploration of her firstborn son's death and its impact on her family and her deeply-held faith, the true purpose of memoir is revealed. Yaffa mines the depth of her experience as a Jew, a wife, and a bereaved mother to paint a shimmering portrait of an existence in complete disarray as she questions everything she knows and believes. She arrives at her explored truths in ways that leave her both brittle and soft, but retaining her unique traits: intelligent, spiritual, mindful and reflective, attuned to her surviving family, her relationship with God, and with her son Dov ever nearby."

—**Gabriella Burman, author of** *"Michaela"*

The
Broken
Vase

A MEMOIR

Yaffa Klugerman

Storytellers Publishing
Colorado, U.S.A.

Storytellers Publishing
An imprint of Journey Institute Press,
a division of 50 in 52 Journey, Inc.
journeyinstitutepress.org

Library of Congress Control Number: Available Upon Request
Names: Klugerman, Yaffa
Title: The Broken Vase
Description: Colorado: Storytellers Publishing, 2025
Identifiers: ISBN 978-1-964754-32-1 (hardcover)
ISBN 978-1-964754-34-5 (paperback)
ISBN 978-1-964754-33-8 (ebook/kindle)
Subjects: BISAC:
BIOGRAPHY & AUTOBIOGRAPHY / Women |
BIOGRAPHY & AUTOBIOGRAPHY / Memoirs |
BIOGRAPHY & AUTOBIOGRAPHY / Jewish

First Edition
Printed in the United States of America

1 6 7 10 19 28 29 44 56 72

This book was typeset in EB Garamond / Amo Pro

Cover design by WiggleB Studios

Contents

Author's Note

The story that you are about to read is true, and is based on a journal I kept during the year after my son Dov suddenly passed away. I have recreated many conversations from memory, and occasionally I have taken some editorial license in their retelling, but they all took place. All the people mentioned are real; however, I have changed or withheld the names of some who preferred not to be identified.

This book is told from my perspective and focuses primarily on my own experience. While my children were certainly dealing with grief and trauma, I chose to respect their privacy by focusing primarily on my own.

Introduction

I'll never forget that phone call.

I'll never forget the sound of the siren in the background, the voice of my sister: *"Call everyone in the family. Dovie's been hit by a car."*

For as long as I can remember, my life has been framed by what I lovingly call "the voice of Yaffa." As a child sharing a room with my sister, that voice was the nagging, annoying, clean-your-room and make-your-bed voice. As I grew, it was the voice of advice, the wisdom of an older sister who navigated life a few years ahead of me and could dole out wisdom like a sage on a mountaintop. Sometimes I appreciated it. Oftentimes not. But as an adult, I knew that whatever problem I had, I could call my older sister and she would have something to say that would guide me.

It was a typical day at the end of May. Summer was approaching. Kids were itching to get out of their classrooms and head to the parks as the school year wound down. The skies were sunny and blue. On that beautiful day, a car barrelled down Arcola Avenue just as Dovie stepped into the street, forever changing the lives of everyone who knew him.

The week after, as he lingered between life and death, I watched from afar, struggling to find the words to comfort Yaffa and her family. There were no words, though. No magic spell to take away the pain or the absolute devastation of the moment when her child passed. In the hierarchy of traumatic experiences, losing a child is probably the highest on the list. It is the nightmare no parent ever wants to endure, and there are no pearls of wisdom adequate enough to comfort the bereaved.

I remember when Yaffa and her family came to visit me a few months after Dovie died. I went to pick them up at the airport, and as I pulled up to the curb, my heart stopped. I saw them—a beautiful family—but was keenly aware of the missing space in their small group. I felt the loss in a way no one on the street could feel. It was the silent touch of grief and mourning that passersby cannot fathom hovering on the faces of a family standing outside an airport gate in sunny Florida. I saw that hole, that aching emptiness, and I didn't know how I could help her fill it. I needed the voice of Yaffa to guide me, but it was not there. Not then. And so I could only hold space for her and her family and stand watch as they navigated their lives through the shattering aftermath of that day in May.

It has been many years since that phone call. I remember it every year the same way I remember the anniversary of Dovie's death. It became an absolute demarcation for the new life I watched my sister build from the rubble of the accident. I was merely a voyeur those years, holding her hand when I could and marveling at how she and her husband Tzvi dedicated themselves to ensuring their family would not fall apart—making sure they found a way to carry on living.

When she handed me this manuscript, I had to read it twice. The first time, I read it as memory, sobbing through the familiar pieces of those days that remain seared into my brain. The second time, I read it with a more critical eye. The story unfolded in a context I had never known—the backstory of split-second decisions made in a hospital room, the perspective of a mother eulogizing her oldest son, the long days of recovery, the silent process that no one else sees. These were the stories I missed, the ones that took place in the private moments of grief. They are raw and real and humbling. I once thought I was meant to fill a hole in my sister's heart, but I learned that grief does not disappear; one must find a way to build a bridge across it.

This memoir, the story of a year following a horrific tragedy, is more than a story of devastation and grief, of the unthinkable and the unimaginable. It is a story of triumph and recovery. Of life in the face of a monstrous death. It is a reminder of the power of living despite tragedy, of facing questions without answers, and somehow finding acceptance, forging a path forward on the tenuous bridge that spans the pit of loss, death, and memory.

The voice of Yaffa was—and still is—a strong guide in my life. When my own family faced difficult times, my children asked me how we would survive. I told them we had role models in our lives who gave us the tools and taught us how to approach challenges with strength and fortitude. We had the voice of Yaffa.

And now, through this book, you have it too.

Adina Ciment
January 2025

Part 1

Chapter 1
Wednesday, May 31, 2006, 4:15 pm

I am standing in the front hall of my house, surrounded by dozens of plastic grocery bags overflowing with food for the holiday of Shavuot, which begins tomorrow night. The custom is to serve dairy, and the bags contain a hearty amount of produce and a variety of cheeses so that I can concoct a blintz soufflé and cherry cheesecake—new recipes both. My son Noam, who has just turned eight, was supposed to help me bring all the groceries in, but he was too involved with his after-school snack to pay me any attention. He is sitting in the kitchen with my youngest son, Avichai, who is four, happily dunking his cinnamon graham crackers into milk while watching TV. Outside, I hear the whirr of the lawn mower as our gardener trims our lawn, a result of my earlier call pleading with him to come, since we are expecting guests, and I fear the grass is beginning to look like an overgrown field. It is a beautiful sunny May afternoon in Maryland.

"Ma'am," the air conditioner repairman says, "your son is lying in the middle of the street."

The air conditioner repairman is also here because of my pleas; our cooling system is not working efficiently, and I want it taken care of before the holiday. For a second, surrounded by the ordinary chaos that precedes any Jewish holiday, I do not comprehend the meaning of his words.

What can he mean? Hillel should be on the school bus coming home, and my other children, Sarit and Dov, should still be in class. And then, suddenly, I bolt out the door and run.

Almost directly in front of our house, traffic has come to a complete stop. People—mostly teachers and students from the school across the street—have surrounded the scene. There must be noise, but I hear nothing at all. Sprawled on the black pavement lies a boy not yet fifteen, dressed in black pants and a button-down pinstriped shirt, clothes I ran out to buy for him several months ago at JC Penney when he realized he had nothing to wear that would conform to the dress code of his new school. As I draw closer, my throat constricts and my breathing changes to short, rapid gasps, and I am certain I am in a nightmare, viewing the scene from someone else's eyes. At any second, surely, I will wake up. I blink, fully expecting to find myself in bed, but instead I see the same scene in front of me. The same boy is lying, still, on the pavement.

It is Dov. My eldest son.

I know I should be screaming, but I cannot. I can barely talk. I can barely breathe. I see a car stopped about fifty feet from Dov, its driver visibly shaken. "He came out of nowhere!" she cries. Later, I will be unable to remember what she looked like, only that she was female. I draw closer to Dov and kneel at his side. He is breathing heavily, moaning. His eyes are closed. I see a trickle of blood flowing from his ear.

"The ambulance is on the way," says one of Dov's teachers. He is standing nearby, but he sounds distant, as if he is on the other side of the world. All I am aware of is the breathing; Dov's deep gulps of air as he moans, my quick gasps as my heart races. Inhale, exhale, over and over again, as slowly my brain begins to comprehend that what I am seeing is indeed real. This is no nightmare.

Finally, I find my voice. "I need a phone," I say, and the teacher hands one to me. I dial my husband's cell phone and cannot get through. I call my neighbor, Judy Rosenthal, who lives across the street, and her husband Stuart picks up.

"Is Judy there?" I ask him.

"Not at the moment. Can I help?"

Inhale, exhale. "Dov just got hit by a car."

"Oh my goodness!"

"I need someone to watch my kids," I say. "Can you please—"

"I'm leaving right now."

In the corner of my eye, I see Stuart darting across the street. I try my husband again. This time I get through.

"Tzvi..." I gasp, and then my voice breaks. I simply cannot get the words out. I cannot articulate the horror. The terror.

"I heard. I'm coming."

"Tzvi!" I cry, because his name is the only word I can muster.

"I'm coming."

The phone clicks and I hand it back to the teacher. Now I kneel by Dov and hold his hand. Someone tells me to talk to him. If this were the movies, I would be screaming and holding him in my arms, begging him to be strong. But words elude me. What can I possibly say?

"Dov," I finally tell him, with great effort, leaning towards his ear, "I am here. The ambulance is on the way. I love you, and I am with you. Hold on, Dov, hold on."

The old CPR training I once learned kicks in instinctively, and I take his pulse. His heart is beating—a strong, vibrant pulse. Later, I wonder. Why did I take his pulse? He was breathing. You don't take a pulse when someone is breathing. I do it now because I think that there must be something I am supposed to do. There must be something I am supposed to say. I sit helplessly by my wounded son, who has now stopped moaning, and I feel his pulse, and I wait for help to arrive.

"His name..." says the teacher.

I look at him, confused. He knows Dov's name.

"Dov ben Yaffa?" he asks.

I nod silently, but I don't understand why he is asking me.

At one point, I raise my head and spot Noam, standing on our front lawn, watching the commotion, and instinctively I want to shield him from the trauma that is taking place right in front of our home. It is bad enough that I am seeing it. I will not tolerate my children seeing it.

"Noam!" I scream. "Get back inside the house!"

I watch him leave. The ambulance arrives and the paramedics begin to work on Dov. I feel my mind beginning to function again, and I realize I need to fetch my purse if I am to accompany the ambulance. "Stay here," I tell the teacher. "Don't let them leave without me."

I run back to my house and grab my purse. "Can you watch my kids?" I ask Stuart.

"Go!" he urges. "Just go!"

In a moment of clarity within so much confusion, I hand him my car keys; my car will need to be moved so the gardener and air conditioning repairman can exit my driveway. Later, I will realize that this was the first clear sign that I was beginning to think again.

I bolt out the door for the second time that day. The paramedics are loading Dov into the ambulance. "I'm coming with you," I tell the driver, who motions for me to join him in the front.

And then suddenly I realize what the teacher was asking me. He wants to know Dov's Hebrew name so the school can pray for him.

"His name..." I call to him.

"Yes?"

"Dov Matityahu ben Yaffa Yehudit." The teachers begin to repeat the name over and over, so as not to forget, switching my Sephardic pronunciation to an Ashkenazic one. "Dov Matisyahu ben Yaffa Yehudis. Dov Matisyahu ben Yaffa Yehudis."

I can hear them reciting his name as I close the door to the ambulance and we drive away.

Chapter 2
Spring 1999

Seven years earlier, I had gone to see the house at 1215 Arcola Avenue for the first time. The real estate agent was supposed to meet me at three, but she was a few minutes late, so I stood in front of the house and took in my surroundings. The house was begging for a decent coat of paint, and leaves covered every inch of the lawn—assuming, of course, that there was a lawn. I really couldn't say for sure. But what made the greatest impression was not what I saw, but what I heard: traffic, lots of it, passing directly in front of the house, scattering the leaves everywhere. Was the force of the traffic actually loosening the paint on the house?

As I observed the cars, trucks, buses, and ambulances passing by, I realized I was wasting my time. Why would anyone live here, in the middle of a main street, when most of the Kemp Mill community of Silver Spring, Maryland, could be found lining quiet, tranquil roads?

"Sorry I'm late," said the agent, when she eventually pulled up. "The keys are right in the lockbox over there." I was almost inclined to tell her to forget it and go home, but despite my misgivings, I waited with her as she fiddled with the lock. After what seemed like a great struggle, she managed to turn the key, and then we stepped inside.

I was taken aback by what I saw. Shiny, white ceramic tiles lined the foyer and powder room. The baseboards and coat closet were painted mauve—the exact color of our sofas. The living room was enormous, with a high ceiling and a beautiful, finished wood floor. A large bay window overlooked Arcola Avenue. When I saw it, an unbidden thought popped into my head: *What a marvelous windowsill for the menorahs!* The dining room was tiny, but we could easily use the large front room instead, which was currently a den.

I stepped into the kitchen and stifled a gasp. It was roughly twice the size of the kitchen in the house that we were renting. There were endless stretches of new, wooden cabinets, easily enough to hold our dairy, meat, and Passover dishes. There was a self-cleaning double oven and one large stainless-steel sink—easy to make kosher. A stove with five gas burners. And—the ultimate luxury—two dishwashers, one for dairy, and one for meat.

"The former owners made a lot of renovations to this house," explained the agent. "I guess you can tell that this was a kosher kitchen."

"It's fabulous," I gushed.

"It's a beautiful kitchen," she agreed, "with room for everything."

The kitchen windows had an eastern exposure and overlooked the spacious backyard. I imagined having breakfast with our children in a room bathed in sunlight. I noticed that the back door led directly onto a new wooden deck, and one of the kitchen windows peered directly onto it. *The perfect place for a sukkah.* I pictured serving food through the window to guests outside.

"Where are the former owners?" I asked.

"They no longer live here. They put in these expensive renovations, but when the real estate market tanked, they couldn't sell the house for what they needed to repay their loans, so it went into foreclosure. It's been unoccupied for two years."

I was incredulous. "You mean nobody wanted to buy this house?"

"It was a tough market back then, but things are just picking up now. I expect this will sell quickly."

I explored the rest of the house, taking my time. Room by room, I found every feature I had ever hoped for in a home. A master bedroom with enough room for our ornate wood bedroom set, with its own adjoining bathroom. Three other bedrooms for the four children we had then. A carpeted rec room downstairs where the children could play. Enough wall space to fit Tzvi's extensive library of books on Judaism, Jewish law, and philosophy. Two additional bedrooms in the basement, one with a private bathroom; perfect, I thought, for a study and a guest bedroom for when my parents or in-laws visited. And there was even room to expand—should we need to—in the basement.

"You might want to do something about all the ceiling fans," the agent remarked.

Every bedroom contained a ceiling fan, and there were two in the kitchen. "No," I replied, thinking of Tzvi's tendency to sweat in temperatures above forty degrees, "we actually love ceiling fans."

It seemed too good to be true. I had expected that the first house we bought would be small, a long walk from the nearest shul, and that it would take years for us to renovate it. Here was a large house, already painted in colors that matched our furniture, with a brand new, huge kitchen, four bathrooms, and it was actually affordable. It had *two* dishwashers. Who would have ever thought we might be able to have that?

"The real question you have to ask yourself," said the agent, "is, can you live with this?" She gestured toward the bay window overlooking Arcola Avenue, where the traffic sped by directly in front of the house. "That's something you have to decide. Because I really believe that if you can deal with living on a main street, you will be very happy here."

I wasn't sure I *would* be able to deal with it. I was conscious of the constant rush of vehicles, which could be heard throughout the house. We were renting a house on a street far away from the bustle of commuters and shoppers, where we drifted off to sleep hearing the hum of crickets and cicadas and woke up to the harmonious trills of birds. I thought of my childhood home on a cul-de-sac, where I had played kick-the-can on our street and rode bikes with my siblings and the neighborhood kids for hours until our parents had to remind us to come in for dinner. If we bought this house, our children would grow up in very different surroundings.

I realized, however, that this was what was available, and the market was taking off, so prices were rising. A house this size, in this condition, at this price, and in such close proximity to a shul was very likely the best deal that we would find.

I went home, pondered the pros and cons, and told Tzvi about the house. I went back with him a few days later. He was excited and ready to buy the house as soon as he saw it, but still I hesitated. There was something about it that didn't feel right.

Judy, who lived across the street, had two children who were in the same grades as Sarit and Hillel. I barely knew her at the time, but I spoke to her about what it was like to live on Arcola Avenue. She, her husband, and two children were happy there, she told me, and would be thrilled if we moved onto the street.

"What concerns you about living here?" she asked.

"The noise, obviously," I said. "I'm afraid I won't be able to sleep. What else should concern me?"

"Well, many people are afraid that their kids will run into the street."

That seemed like an overblown fear to me. "I'm not worried about that," I replied. "My kids know not to run into the street. Even when we lived on streets with barely any traffic, they knew not to go in the street. Besides, plenty of children have grown up safely on busy streets."

"I agree with you. I'm just telling you what people say."

Still, I couldn't make up my mind. I knocked on the door of the white-haired woman next door, who had raised nine children in her home. I explained some of my concerns.

"The traffic is terrible," she agreed. "It's gotten much worse since we moved here thirty years ago. If I ever move, that would be the reason. But it's a nice place to live. The park across the street is wonderful for the children. And they can go bike riding on the bike path behind the supermarket.

"But one thing I should tell you," she added. "You should cross at the corner, and tell your children to cross at the corner too."

A few days later, I drove back to 1215 Arcola Avenue and walked into the leaf-covered backyard. I sat on the deck and listened to the birds' chirps mingling with the rush of traffic passing by in front of the house. *Can I live with this?* I asked myself. *Can I live with this?*

After several weeks of deliberating, I decided that I could. Yet still, I hesitated at every stage of the sale. We arranged a home inspection and I found myself hoping that some major repair would be detected so that the deal would fall through. Several houses went up for sale nearby, and I found myself wondering if I should go and take a look, just to make sure I didn't like anything else better. I worried about paying the mortgage. I worried that my children would never get used to the noise. I worried that if we ever needed to sell the house, we would not be able to. I worried until we closed on the house and began to move in, and then once we were settled, I became convinced that we had made the biggest mistake of our lives.

"This was a bad idea," I told my younger sister, Adina Ciment, who lived in Miami Beach. "I think I've really screwed up this time. I don't think we'll sell this house if we ever put it on the market."

"Yaffa," said Adina, who never hesitated to speak her mind, "there's a term for that: buyer's remorse. But you are crazy, do you know that? You have a new house. Enjoy it and shut up!"

Guests visited and told us we were so fortunate to buy such a beautiful and large house in foreclosure. My in-laws were especially proud that Tzvi, who worked at the time as a teacher, and I, then a youth group director, had saved enough money to pay for the house by ourselves. My mother thought the kitchen was a dream.

Only I could not come to terms with it. At night, I tossed and turned when I heard the traffic, certain that I would never sleep soundly again. I could not think of any rational reason why the house troubled me so much. It was a beautiful house. We lived comfortably. The market took off and the house doubled in value. Logically, I should have been happy. But a tiny voice inside me kept whispering that something was not quite right.

Chapter 3
Wednesday, May 31, 2006, 4:35 pm

As we pull up to DC Children's National Hospital, it appears as if an army of doctors and nurses has assembled to meet us. The ambulance driver tells me not to look as they take Dov out.

"Easy, now," he says, putting a hand on my shoulder. "They've intubated him. I don't want you to pass out."

I look at him as if he has lost his mind. "If I haven't passed out yet," I tell him, nearly clenching my teeth as I speak, "then I'm not going to."

But the sight of Dov being given oxygen does shake me. On the way to the hospital, I had made a single phone call to my sister Adina, asking her to alert the family and to tell everyone to pray. In my panic, I had forgotten that Adina is in her ninth month of pregnancy, and this might not be the best news for her to hear in her state. But it seems that she has done what I asked; everyone knows. My cell phone rings incessantly. I am the second of nine siblings, and they and my parents are all probably trying to reach me. I ignore it; there's nothing else to tell.

They wheel Dov into the Emergency Room, and I am directed to a small room where a social worker is waiting for me. I suddenly realize that my throat is parched with thirst, and she brings me a cup of water and tells me to sit. For the first time, I notice the blood on my sleeve: Dov's blood.

"We had three accidents like this last week," the social worker tells me, "and everyone went home fine."

I realize she is trying hard to reassure me. I drink my water and try to be calm. *He will be okay*, I tell myself.

"Those are normal sounds we are hearing from in there," she says. "Everything sounds as it should."

Tzvi arrives and I meet him in the hall. His eyes reflect my fear. We look through the window to the room and see that they are taking Dov off the spinal backboard. "That's a good sign," says Tzvi, who now works as a middle school principal and was once an Emergency Medical Technician in college. "They're taking him off the board. That's good."

"Mr. and Mrs. Klugerman, if I can have a word?"

It's the doctor who has been attending Dov. We return to the room with the social worker and sit down with him. *Here is when they tell us that he has been injured, but he will be okay*, I think.

"Mr. and Mrs. Klugerman," says the doctor, "your son has sustained a non-survivable injury. There is nothing we can do for him."

I begin to tremble uncontrollably. Once again, I have the urge to scream, but I cannot. I want to cry, but no sound rises from my throat. What I am hearing is inconceivable. I look at the social worker who had just assured me that things would be fine. She looks stunned. Indeed, it should have taken perhaps a second or two to process the complete meaning of the doctor's words, but those seconds seem to stretch out in slow motion.

Finally, Tzvi finds his voice. "What do you mean, there's nothing you can do for him? Do you mean we're just going to *let him die*? There has to be *something* we can do!"

"No, I'm afraid not," the doctor replies. "I'm sorry. Your son has sustained a serious blow to his head. He is no longer breathing on his own. Our preliminary assessment indicates no brain activity. We can keep him on life support for twenty-four hours, but after that time, if he is still brain dead, we are legally required to turn off life support."

Tears stream down Tzvi's cheeks. "There must be *something* we can do!" he repeats.

"I have never seen anyone survive an injury like this," says the doctor. "I am sorry."

My voice shakes as I speak. "Can we see him?"

"Yes, of course, for a few minutes."

We walk into the next room and see Dov breathing through a respirator. *Less than two hours ago he was fine. How can this be happening?*

"Dov," says Tzvi, in a voice I've never heard, "it's Daddy. You've been hurt, but you need to fight. Do you hear me? Fight like you've never fought before! Fight for your life! *Fight for your life*! Don't give up, Dov, don't give up! We love you and we need you to fight!"

I am still having trouble finding my voice. "Dovie," I say softly, "we love you. We want you to get better. Don't give up. We are with you and praying for you."

The nurses motion for us to step out as they prepare Dov to move to the intensive care unit. Alone for a few minutes in a side room, I finally call Adina.

"Yaffa! Talk to me!"

I start to cry. "Oh Adina, it's bad. It's really bad. He has a head injury."

"What did the doctors tell you?"

"They said...they said...that they don't think he'll survive."

I can hear her gasp. "They told you that?"

"Yes," I tell her, wiping my tears. "That's what they said. There's no brain activity, and they think it's a matter of time. Listen to me, okay? Don't tell anyone. I'm afraid people will give up hope, and we need them to keep praying. Do you understand? Tell them to keep praying for him."

I can't believe this. I just can't believe it. Just a few hours ago, he was fine. I was getting ready for the holiday. He was planning to go to camp. "Oh God! Adina!" I cry in anguish. "I wish...I wish I could just delete the day."

I hang up and walk back to where Tzvi is sitting, head in his hands. Standing by his side is Dr. Dan Feldman, our beloved pediatrician, who heard what happened and left his office to check on us. Just two weeks ago, Dov saw him for his annual check-up. I remember the two of them arguing about a tetanus shot. Dr. Feldman had no record of him receiving one recently, but Dov was certain he had.

"I have a good memory," Dov had said adamantly. "I definitely had that shot. And I don't want a shot that I don't need."

"Dov, there would be a record of it if you had it," I had reasoned.

"The records are wrong," he insisted, in typical teenage-know-it-all fashion. "I remember that shot."

Dr. Feldman had known Dov for almost a decade, and he also knew better than to argue. "Okay, look, let's try this. Maybe when they switched all the records to computer, they somehow forgot to include that shot. I'm willing to go to the storeroom and check the written records. But if I find that it's not mentioned there either, you'll have to get that shot."

Dov frowned but knew the deal was a fair one. "Fine. You'll see. I remember that shot."

We waited in the examining room while Dr. Feldman went down the hall to unlock the records. I pictured him entering a storeroom similar to the one housing the Ark of the Covenant in *Raiders of the Lost Ark*. Together, Dov and I sat silently, waiting for his return.

After what seemed like a very long time, Dr. Feldman returned. "Well, I wouldn't have believed it..."

"Yes?" said Dov, his eyes lighting up.

"You were right. You had that shot just a few years ago, and somehow it wasn't transferred onto the computer records."

"I knew it!" yelled Dov. "You see, Mom? I was right!"

I think of that tetanus shot as I face Dr. Feldman now in the hospital. Dark-haired, kind, cool Dr. Feldman, who has always known what to say and how to say it, who listened patiently to my concerns about fevers, ear infections, fine motor issues, and bedwetting, and who always reassured me, with a twinkle in his eye, that kids get into trouble, and yes, they get sick, but that most get through it all and grow up just fine. This same man is standing next to Tzvi now, and he is looking at me with no reassurance in his gaze. The twinkle in his eye is gone, and he has nothing to say. There is absolutely nothing any of us can say.

Chapter 4
Life on Arcola

The best part about living on Arcola Avenue was the location. We were situated on the main thoroughfare of the Kemp Mill Jewish community, two large synagogues sandwiching us like bookends to the west and east. Both were important to us; we prayed regularly at the Young Israel Shomrai Emunah, and the Silver Spring Jewish Center housed the community mikvah. We could get up five minutes before services began and make it to shul on time. Our children learned to cross the street by the specially programmed light that allowed hundreds of Shabbat observers to cross without pressing any buttons; the light was the only one in the county which stopped traffic in all four directions so pedestrians could actually cross diagonally. Our shul became our second home; we went not only for services, but for youth programs, clothing sales, dinners, and bnei mitzvah parties.

The Yeshiva of Greater Washington's middle and high school for boys was located directly across the street. Right next to it was the Kemp Mill Park. This was where I pushed my children on swings, where they later went to play basketball, where Dov learned to ride a bicycle, his light brown hair blown by the wind as he circled the pond and dodged the obnoxious geese and ducks that made their home there. Beyond the park lay the Kemp Mill Shopping Center, where our dentist and doctor practiced and where one could visit a kosher pizza place, a kosher bakery, a kosher butcher, a drugstore, dry cleaner, and supermarket. Behind the supermarket snaked a bike path which led to Sligo Creek Parkway and beyond, with numerous playgrounds and wildlife along the way. This is where we walked on Rosh Hashanah for *tashlich*, throwing bread into a brook and asking God to forgive our sins. One year, Dov and I spent Sunday mornings riding bikes together, just the two of us, along that path.

On Chanukah, we would gather with our children to light our menorahs in our front window and wave to the Yeshiva students across the street who were lighting theirs. Each one of us had our own menorah, ranging from sterling silver to handmade wooden blocks with bolts for candle holders, but there was room for them all on our generous front windowsill. Sometimes, on Shabbat afternoons, I would sit by that window and watch the hundreds of Jews who would stroll by our house, on their way to visit friends, attend classes, or pray. We were living in the very heart of our community, and on Shabbat afternoons in particular, we rarely found any reason to leave our street.

In the winter, ours was the first street to be plowed. We often mocked the county for closing the schools because of the snow, because we truly didn't have a clue how treacherous other streets were. In the spring, the cherry trees lining Arcola bloomed with thousands of beautiful blossoms. One year, a woodpecker settled just above our bedroom window and began to peck at precisely six fifteen every morning. Another year, several chimney swifts moved into our chimney, and we spent the season listening to them raising their family.

We not only lived in the heart of the Jewish community, but close to the rich array of public buildings, parks, and services that Kemp Mill offered its residents. Further down Arcola Avenue was the Wheaton Ice Rink. Sarit took lessons for years, and in winter, when the snow was just right, we would take all our children there to sled down the hills that surrounded it. Further still, by the intersection of Georgia Avenue, was the public library that we visited regularly, and beyond that, Wheaton Regional

Park and the magnificent Brookside Gardens, where we once posed for a family portrait that still adorns our front hall.

The worst part about living on Arcola Avenue was the location. Four lanes of traffic passed in front of our house every minute of the day and for a good part of the night. When we moved in, I was sure I would quickly become accustomed to the constant hum of vehicles traveling down the street, but many months passed before I could effectively drown out the noise.

"It's like the ocean," suggested a neighbor of mine, trying to put a positive spin on the din, but I could not hear it as anything other than traffic. I frequently chose to sit in the kitchen, where the sound was muffled, so I didn't have to think about it, but it was never far from my awareness. Especially at night, when I longed to feel a cool breeze, but could only hear the rushing air of passing vehicles.

Garbage regularly appeared on our front lawn. One day, an entire album full of heavy-metal CDs somehow materialized in front of our house; I was never able to find the owner. At the edge of our driveway, I frequently discovered dozens of cigarette butts. Initially, I wondered if groups of people actually stood smoking in front of our house late at night, but I later realized that these, along with the garbage, had been thrown from passing cars.

We were highly visible. I couldn't bring in the newspaper if I was not fully dressed; it felt as if the entire Yeshiva was watching. When our lawn wasn't immaculately kept, it felt like the entire community would notice. I made a habit of cleaning up the stray garbage that constantly migrated over our property line. When we had plumbing problems, friends and neighbors would spot the truck in our driveway and inquire as to what was going on. At night, I always drew the shades, because otherwise everyone could see what we were doing. When our gardener mistakenly showed up on a *yom tov* to mow our lawn, I was horrified and humiliated; it seemed as if everyone must have witnessed our gaffe.

We learned early on that some people were so afraid of the street that they would not drive on it at all. We coined a term for this phenomenon: Arcolaphobia. It was not an altogether unfounded fear; there were many fender-benders on our street, though none were life-threatening. When we first moved in, before we extended our driveway, I told Tzvi we could legally park in front of our house on the street, but I changed my mind about actually doing so when I saw someone drive down the road one night and plow into a parked car, not at all expecting anything to be there.

And yet, I didn't fear for our lives. Plenty of people grow up on busy streets, I told myself. We just had to be careful—and so we were. Our children learned at an early age to stay away from the road. When we installed a basketball hoop in our driveway, we taught our kids not to run after the ball if it bounced into the street. When they played outside, I stood on the edge of the driveway and kept watch, making sure that no scooters, balls, bikes, or play cars left our property. When they rode bikes on the sidewalk, I ran alongside them to make sure they didn't steer out of control. Vigilance became a way of life.

Still, I truly never saw Arcola as a dangerous street. I witnessed traffic slowing to allow geese and ducks to cross. Cars would screech to a halt when a ball bounced into the street. On Arcola, everyone crossed in the middle of the street: Our neighbors, Barbara and Clif Price, boarded two Yeshiva students, and they regularly hopped across Arcola to get to school. Down the block, Dov's friends did the same. Yeshiva students parked in front of our house and crossed the street to get to class on time. In fact, my backyard neighbor fenced in her yard to *prevent* Yeshiva students from cutting through to cross in front of our house. Down the block, residents of a group home for adults with mental disabilities regularly cut across Arcola to walk to the Kemp Mill Shopping Center. On Shabbat, I would see dozens of mothers pushing their strollers across the middle of Arcola to reach the playground.

So I saw absolutely no danger. I was absolutely not concerned. I was particularly unconcerned about Dov, who I thought was arguably one of the most careful children who had ever lived. In the mornings, Tzvi would watch him from the window as he crossed the road to the Yeshiva. Dov would stand at the curb cautiously, clutching his rolling backpack. Even though he was usually running late, he would look to the left and then to the right. And then he would look to the left again. If all was clear, he would proceed across the street. Day after day, evening after evening, he went through the same routine. When he needed to meet with a tutor during the day, we arranged with the school to allow him to cross the street and return home so they would have a quiet place to work together. When he had an afternoon break, he would sometimes come home to grab a snack. So confident was I in his ability to cross the road that one day, after navigating the crowded parking lot at the Yeshiva to pick him up for a doctor's appointment, I suggested to Dov that it would be far easier for him to simply come home so I could take him from there.

Later, after the accident, I would wonder, weeping, why I did not insist that he cross at the corner, where there was a crosswalk. And I realized that the answer, quite simply, was that it had never even occurred to me. We lived directly across the street from the Yeshiva, and he was a responsible, careful kid. I would fight with him about watching inappropriate DVDs and movies, we would argue about video games and Internet controls, and I would worry about him eating and sleeping enough, making enough friends, using deodorant, and doing homework. I would worry about his safety going skiing, sledding, and biking. But never once, in all the years that we lived on Arcola Avenue, would it ever occur to me to worry about him crossing the street.

Chapter 5
Thursday, June 1, 2006, 5:00 am

The hospital staff, clearly aware of the severity of Dov's injuries, have given us exclusive use of the ICU waiting room. Tzvi is staying close to Dov. I have tossed and turned all night and now, at 5 am, I wonder if I might be able to finally fall asleep, even if only for a short time. Perhaps, I think, if I go to sleep, then when I wake up, everything will be fine. So I stretch out on the chairs, shut the light, and attempt to close my eyes. To no avail. I cannot possibly sleep when I know that just down the hall, my son is hooked up to a respirator, his brain swelling after being injured crossing the street in front of our house.

My mind wanders to my mother-in-law. Yesterday evening, once Dov was admitted to the intensive care unit, Tzvi and I had considered how we should break the news to her. Mom, Francine Klugerman, has been living alone in her house in Brooklyn since my father-in-law passed away four years ago. She is a former parole officer, strong-willed, opinionated, and extremely proud, although her health problems have made it difficult for her to walk in recent years. Tzvi is an only child, and Dov, our oldest, is the apple of his grandmother's eye. She babysat him for the first two years of his life while I worked full time for a publishing house in New York City. I remember her positioning him by our front window every evening. I would see his then-blonde curls bobbing with his excitement as he spotted me arriving home. We didn't know how to break such catastrophic news over the phone, worried that if she were to collapse in anguish, nobody would be there to care for her. Finally, we decided to call her rabbi and explain the situation, and he arranged for someone in the community to wait near her house in case she needed assistance after receiving our call. Once the details were arranged, Tzvi sat down and slowly dialed her number.

"Mom," he said, his voice breaking, "there's been a terrible accident."

I remember her crying as Tzvi broke the news. She assured us that she would drive to the hospital, nearly five hours away, early the next morning. When we told her that someone was waiting outside if she needed a hand to hold, she shrugged it off and told us, once again, that she would arrive as soon as she could. I wonder if she is already setting out.

I really should be praying. I look forlornly at the stack of siddurim and books of Tehillim that my brother Ari and his wife Deena brought us when they drove in yesterday from their home in nearby Baltimore. Others had joined us as well: Rabbis from the Yeshiva related to us that word had spread quickly throughout the community about Dov's accident. Hundreds had crowded together in our synagogue to pray for Dov. "The shul was packed," one of Dov's teachers had reported. "It was standing room only."

Rabbi Gedalia Anemer, the rabbi of Young Israel Shomrai Emunah, had reassured us when we asked him to encourage people to pray for Dovie. "We will demand prayer," he said.

But all our visitors left eventually, and Tzvi and I have been alone with our thoughts and fears for hours in this wretched waiting room, completely powerless to do anything to help Dov, who struggles to hold on to life just down the hall.

The phone's ring startles me. "Yaffa, it's Ema," says my mother, D'vorah Weiss, calling from her house in Connecticut. She and my father, Rabbi Mordechai Weiss, had originally planned to arrive late in the afternoon to spend the holiday with us; instead, they have bumped up their flight and plan to arrive in the hospital early in the morning.

"I have some encouraging news," she tells me. "Yoni was able to speak with Rav Eliyahu's assistant."

My brother Yoni, the youngest of my siblings at age twenty-one, lives in Israel. He has a connection to the renowned Rabbi Mordechai Eliyahu, the former chief rabbi of Israel, and has been working furiously to be granted an audience.

"And?"

"Rav Eliyahu says to do the following: Have your mezuzahs checked immediately by a *sofer*. Then have him call Rav Eliyahu to explain what was found. He also says that you should do *kapparos* for Dov. Give some *tzedakah*, wave it around Dov's head; do the entire ritual. Also, he said it is important that you give *tzedakah* to Torah institutions. Are you getting all this?"

I am writing down the details in the dark. "Just a minute." The mezuzahs, scrolls fastened to every doorpost in our house, need to be checked by a scribe. We need to perform a ritual of atonement for Dov usually done prior to Yom Kippur, the holiest day of the year. And we must give charitable donations to religious Jewish schools.

"Also, have the *sofer* check Dov's tefillin. And there's one more thing. You need to get this done immediately. Israel is seven hours ahead, and Shavuot begins this evening, so there's only a small window of time when you will actually be able to reach Rav Eliyahu to tell him about the condition of the mezuzahs. Call the *sofer* now."

"Ema, it's five in the morning. I can't call a *sofer* now."

"Yaffa, this is a matter of life and death! Don't wait! *Do it now*! Do you hear me? Do it now!"

I close my eyes. "Okay," I say. "I'll do it."

"Yaffa, don't lose faith. There's still time. You have to keep believing. I love you. Be strong, honey, be strong!"

As is typical in an observant Jewish household, we have mezuzahs affixed to the right side of every doorpost in our house (with the exception of bathroom doors). The mezuzah cases, which range from simple plastic to elaborate sterling silver, house the words of the Shema, one of our holiest prayers, written on parchment. According to tradition, mezuzahs are supposed to guard the members of the house, and the scrolls are clearly not adequately doing the job if something terrible has happened. This is why families going through difficult circumstances will sometimes be advised to have a *sofer*, a scribe, check their mezuzahs.

I remember that Rabbi Raphael Malka is a *sofer*, although I know him more in his role as a *mohel*—he performed the circumcisions of two of our sons, Noam and Avichai. Rabbi Malka is precisely the type of person you want to perform such a delicate operation: His face, framed by his snow-white beard and hair, radiates kindness and good humor, and he cradles the babies with love. Although I have declined to closely watch any circumcision, particularly those of my sons, I have heard Rabbi Malka as he soothes the crying babies. "I know it hurts," he says to them. "I'm so sorry. So sorry."

I tell Tzvi about Rav Eliyahu's instructions and then wake Rabbi Malka before dawn and ask him to please check our mezuzahs as quickly as possible. He agrees immediately, apologizing that he cannot also check the tefillin. Then I wake Judy, our neighbor, who is staying in our house to look after our other children and let her know that Rabbi Malka will be arriving soon. As the sun rises, I am busily making calls, attempting to find someone to check Dov's tefillin.

Tzvi has performed *kapparos*, as instructed, but is dubious about the value of checking tefillin. "Yaffa," he tells me, "we bought those tefillin for Dov less than two years ago, for his bar mitzvah. There's no question that they're kosher."

"What's the harm in checking them?"

"You don't understand. We purchased very high-quality tefillin for him, from Israel. They're not like regular tefillin that can be opened and checked. His tefillin boxes are sealed, because they are expected to be kosher forever. If we want them checked, we have to smash the boxes and pull out the parchment, and then we will need to get them repaired."

I think of Dov down the hall in the ICU and I put my head in my hands. "I am going to find someone to check them," I say, "because I have to know that we tried *everything*. I can't sit here in this room and do nothing. This is the *only thing* that I can do right now which might help. Please, Tzvi, we have to try everything!"

After many, many phone calls, I reach another scribe who agrees to look at Dov's tefillin. Tzvi leaves the hospital, first to attend synagogue for the morning prayers, then to the Yeshiva to fetch Dov's tefillin, to the scribe to check the tefillin, and then back to the hospital.

In the end, we would discover that Dov's tefillin were perfect. Our mezuzahs were kosher, although Rabbi Malka replaced two that looked worn, and added two that he said should have been hung. As the hours pass, and we wait for the doctor to report on Dov's condition—and possibly to tell us he would be disconnected from life support—the waiting room begins to fill with family and friends.

My parents and mother-in-law arrive. We take them to Dovie's room, and I suddenly remember the last time he was in the hospital, as a newborn, the first grandchild on both sides of the family. Back then, I had proudly introduced both my parents and my in-laws to their first grandson; now, I show them the same child, grown to be a young man but grievously injured, hooked up to a ventilator and monitors. It is an awful, heart-wrenching sight.

"Thank God Dad is not alive to see this," my mother-in-law says.

My uncle, Rabbi Avi Weiss, drives in from New York. My older brother, Yitzie Weiss, drives in from New Jersey. Once again, community members deliver kosher food to us, although we cannot possibly eat. Family, friends, and acquaintances surround us, encircle us, all present to provide support and love in an unimaginable and unfathomable situation.

Two doctors arrive. My mother grips my hand. "Be strong," she whispers. "Stand your ground."

I begin to shake uncontrollably.

The older doctor glances around the full waiting room. "Perhaps it would be better if we spoke alone with the parents," he suggests.

Tzvi and I exchange glances and nod. The crowd slowly files out, and the four of us are left alone in the room as we close the door.

"Mr. and Mrs. Klugerman," the doctor begins, "or, forgive me, I understand it's *Rabbi* and Mrs. Klugerman?"

I nod. I am trying hard to stop trembling.

"Well, then, Rabbi and Mrs. Klugerman," continues the doctor, "as you know, Dov sustained a very serious head injury. When he arrived yesterday and we conducted our examination, we were certain that there was no brain activity."

My eyes begin to water. *Say it, already*! I want to scream. *Just get it over with*!

"This morning, when we examined Dov, we were surprised. His breathing showed improvement. And the EEG showed definite signs of higher brain activity. So we are going to monitor him very closely, and do our best to control brain swelling."

Once again, I am speechless, only this time, it is with joy.

"So," Tzvi asks, "there is still hope?"

"There is still hope."

After the doctors leave, we receive a call from Yoni. Rabbi Malka has called Rabbi Eliyahu about the condition of the mezuzahs, and Rabbi Eliyahu asked that a message be relayed to us: "*lo l'natek kloom*." Don't disconnect anything. Regardless of what the doctors say, continue life support.

Chapter 6
February 2006: Dov's Yeshiva

When Dov started learning at the Yeshiva of Greater Washington, across the street from us, it was the first time in our lives that we had sent one of our children to a particular school entirely of our own choice. Our five children had always attended school, obviously, but where they were educated had always depended on where Tzvi was working.

When we lived in Harrisburg, Pennsylvania, they attended the school where he served as high school coordinator. When we moved to Silver Spring, and Tzvi started teaching at what would become the Melvin J. Berman Hebrew Academy, we enrolled our children there as well. By 2006, we had been in Silver Spring for twelve years, and Tzvi had become the middle school principal at MJBHA. Our children accompanied him to school every morning. It wasn't that we ever felt *compelled* to enroll our children in the schools where Tzvi was employed. Quite the contrary; Tzvi only ever considered employment in educational institutions that would be appropriate for our children. It wasn't only a matter of principle, but convenience—and it was certainly far less expensive.

But by 2006, Dov had become unhappy at MJBHA. Although he desperately wanted to excel, he struggled with learning issues. Many of his friends had left the school, so he felt socially isolated. Day after day, I would watch him return from school sullen, dejected, and defeated. Tzvi and I met with

Dov's teachers, who went to great lengths to help him. Yet he was still unhappy.

So even though it was the middle of the school year, we began to look into the possibility of sending him to the Yeshiva. Doing so would be a tremendous change for all of us: Dov would no longer be in a co-ed institution, but at a more yeshivish all-boys' school, his school day would be longer, he would have class on Sundays, and he would be required to conform to a stricter dress code. The increased tuition cost would most definitely put a strain on our budget, and I wasn't quite sure how we would manage it. The decision might also put a strain on Tzvi's standing at MJBHA, as he would have to explain why he was enrolling his son in a competing academic institution.

"We can't worry about that," Tzvi told me when I voiced this concern. "People will adjust. It will be a big surprise at first, but then it will blow over."

"But how will this decision affect you at work?" I asked. "We need to consider that."

"No, we don't. We have to do what's best for our child. That's the most important issue here. Our children must come first."

The Yeshiva presented some very real advantages: Many of Dov's friends from the neighborhood attended there. The classes were much smaller. We hoped Dov could thrive there. Very discreetly, at the end of January, Tzvi contacted the Yeshiva's principal, Rabbi Dovid Niman, and informed him that Dov would like to investigate enrolling. We arranged to have Dov visit the school for two days, and then scheduled an interview with the rabbis. Dov was both excited and nervous.

"How could you send me there?" he asked doubtfully. "I can't deal with going to school on Sundays."

"What exactly do you do on Sundays now? Watch TV?"

"I like my TV."

"You'll manage without it. It's just for a few hours on Sunday."

"But the Yeshiva isn't our type of place."

"You have good friends there."

"But," he said, "it's so religious there."

I smiled. "You'll fit in fine."

"Mom, what if I start wearing a black hat? What will you do then?"

I paused. A black hat, in religious circles, is a statement that you identify with the more "yeshivish" crowd—which could mean, among other things, that you don't socialize with girls, you may not go to movies, and you might be stricter about which kosher certification you accept. Personally, I prefer crocheted yarmulkes, a common indicator of modern Orthodoxy, a fact of which Dov was aware.

"I will be happy," I replied, "if you wearing a black hat is the worst problem we have."

For two days, Dov dressed in a button-down shirt and slacks—quite a contrast to his regular black jeans and polo shirt—and crossed the street to attend classes at the Yeshiva. At first, he merely sat and listened, but at a certain point, he ran back home to fetch a pen and paper.

When he later showed us his notebook, Tzvi and I were incredulous.

"Can you believe it?" I whispered to Tzvi. "He's *taking notes.*"

Dov hadn't taken notes for years. Prior to this experience in the Yeshiva, he would always complain that writing was too difficult for him, and that he couldn't read his own handwriting. We had made accommodations to help him; his teachers would arrange to have notes copied for him, he would type on a device we gave him, and his tests were often given to him orally. We rarely, if ever, saw him with a pen in hand.

For his interview, we advised Dov to wear a suit. He met with the rabbis, who then met with us.

"We don't usually take in kids in the middle of the year," said Rabbi Niman. "But Dov is precisely the type of boy we want in the Yeshiva. We're just not sure where to place him: He could attend the upper-level Talmud class, where he would struggle but be challenged, or he could attend the lower-level class, which would be easier, but he wouldn't be with his friends."

"I think that he should go into the upper-level class," I said. "He wants to learn."

"I'm just concerned that he might become discouraged," said Rabbi Niman.

Tzvi suggested that we ask Dov directly, so we called him into the office.

"Tell me, Dov," said Rabbi Niman, "why do you want to come to the Yeshiva?"

Dov had never been much of a big talker, but he found his voice. "I want to be in a serious Torah atmosphere."

Rabbi Niman smiled. "Are you willing to work hard for that serious Torah atmosphere? Can you manage being in a high-level class, or would you prefer to start in the lower one?"

"I want to try the higher one," he said.

"Very well. Do you have any concerns about coming here?"

Dov thought before replying. "I'm worried I won't be able to handle the long hours."

"The hours are longer, true," said Rabbi Niman, "but you've got to admit that the commute's a lot shorter."

We laughed. Dov could literally roll out of bed and be at school in five minutes.

"But I will tell you one thing very seriously, Dov," Rabbi Niman said. "You should be very careful crossing Arcola Avenue. That street is a dangerous street."

I'm not concerned, I thought.

Chapter 7
Thursday, June 1, 2006, 3:00 pm

Our visitors have all left the hospital, and Tzvi and I need to leave as well. Shavuot will begin in the evening, and we need to get home to shower and pack our bags because we will be spending the holiday in the hospital with Dov. In a flurry of activity, arrangements are made: Mom and my parents will spend the holiday with our other children. Community members, realizing that my parents and mother-in-law are far too traumatized to deal with preparing for the holiday, have already planned their meals. Bikur Cholim of Greater Washington, a local organization that aids the ill, has arranged food for me and Tzvi at the hospital. They will pack up and bring kosher meals to the hospital for us that won't need to be heated, and volunteers have even managed to locate a suitable refrigerator at the hospital for us that will open without a light automatically turning on.

My mother embraces me before she and my father leave for our house. "I have a gift for you," she says. "I didn't know this would happen, but I think you could use this gift now more than ever." She reaches into her bag and pulls out a small blue prayer book, with my name stamped in gold on the cover.

I gaze at the gift and at my name in Hebrew: Yaffa Yehudit. "Thank you, Ema," I say, and I hug her closely. That siddur will soon become my lifeline.

Later, when Tzvi and I arrive home, I find an army of volunteers setting our table and warming up food. I embrace everybody, but I save my warmest hugs for my children. A day has passed since Dovie's accident, and I realize, with some shock, that we haven't spoken with our children in all that time. Our attention has been solely focused on saving Dovie's life, to the point where we have neglected to even wonder what our other children have been going through.

"Avichai," I cry to my four-year-old, "I have missed you."

"Won't you be here for Shavuot?" he asks.

"We wish we could be here. But Dovie is very hurt, and we need to stay with him in the hospital. Grandma, Saba, and Savta will take care of you while we are there."

"Oh," he says, his face falling. "I want you to stay with us."

"We want to be here too," I say honestly, "but we have to stay with Dovie now."

"Will Dovie be all right?" pipes up Hillel, age eleven.

"We hope so," Tzvi answers. "We have to pray that Hashem will make him better."

"Can we see him?" Hillel asks.

"When Shavuot is over, you can visit him in the hospital," I reply.

"What's wrong with Dovie?" asks Avichai.

"He got hit by a car," answers Noam, age eight, who obviously wasn't as shielded from the trauma as I had hoped.

"Ema," says our daughter Sarit, age thirteen, "will I still be able to go on my New York trip?"

I hadn't thought of that. Her much-anticipated eighth-grade trip to New York is next week, and Sarit has been counting the days. A part of me is relieved; despite Dov's accident, she is acting normal.

"We'll have to see how things go," Tzvi answers. "Let's take this one day at a time."

"Sarit," I say, "thank you for helping yesterday. I understand you unloaded all of those groceries I left behind."

"Yeah, well...whatever. I hope Dovie will be okay soon."

I catch myself so my eyes don't fill up with tears. "We all do."

I dash into the shower and pack hurriedly, then grab my suitcase and head downstairs. On the way, I pass Dov's bedroom. Suddenly, I halt in my tracks and gingerly step inside. I gaze at his books, his computer, his bed, the clothes folded on his dresser. An ordinary bedroom for a fourteen-year-old boy. Why isn't he here now? Why isn't he showering and getting ready for the holiday? I feel a sudden wave of anguish and horror, and I abruptly turn on my heel and leave the room, closing the door as I exit.

Together, Tzvi and I embrace our children and parents once again and tell them to keep praying. We will be in touch with them when the holiday ends in two days. We drive away, and I close my eyes as we pass the section of the street where the accident occurred. The police have marked the area with yellow tape, and I cannot bear to see it. I just cannot bear it.

Once we arrive back in the hospital, a social worker guides us to a locker room for parents where we drop off our suitcases and prepare ourselves for the holiday. Not that we have much to do; Bikur Cholim volunteers have handed us instructions telling us where we can find our food and what we will be eating for each meal. They have also provided us with electric candlesticks, so that I can usher in the holiday without fire, which is prohibited in the hospital. Clutching the candlesticks along with my new siddur, I head for the hospital chapel with Tzvi. As we walk through the halls of the hospital, I hear the continuous beeps of medical equipment and notice the high volume of staff on call here. *Children's Hospital is one of the best hospitals in the country. Surely Dov has a good chance of recovery here.*

After I switch on the candlesticks, and Tzvi and I pray, we take the steps down to the cafeteria, to fetch our food. There, a worker leads us to a refrigerator in the back wherein lies a large package of food for us, courtesy of Bikur Cholim. We take our meal upstairs to one of the parent lounges, find a table, and set it with the plasticware provided along with the food. Tzvi recites Kiddush on grape juice, and we wash our hands and eat challah silently. Around us, other parents sit, each trying to deal with their own tragic, heart-wrenching circumstances. From the depths of this hell, Tzvi and I partake of a festive and delicious meal prepared for us with kindness and love. There is not much to say, but we are grateful to have family and friends who are tending to our children so that we can be together.

Our meal done, we head to the ICU to visit Dov. Tzvi brings several *sefarim* with him. Together, we sit by our son and watch the nurses tend to him. The ventilator breathes for him, and a device measures his ICP, which I learn stands for intracranial pressure. These numbers, I have been told, are the ones that indicate the devastation in his brain; the higher the number, the greater the pressure in the skull, and the greater the chance of brain damage. Like anxious brokers watching the stock market, we eye the numbers warily as they rise a few notches and then fall. Tzvi opens one of his books.

"It's Shavuot, Dovie," he says. "It's time to learn Torah."

He begins reading aloud, first the Torah verse, then the commentary on it, speaking to Dov throughout. I am a silent witness to this surreal Torah discourse. The Torah is likened to a tree of life and here, in this bleak intensive care unit, Tzvi's words impart strength, beauty, and hope. I inhale the words of Torah and pray that Dov is somehow doing the same. For several hours we sit this way, until my eyelids begin to droop, and I excuse myself to lie down in a small room designated for the parents of patients. As is the custom on Shavuot, Tzvi intends to spend the whole night learning.

A little after midnight, Tzvi comes to rouse me. "Dov isn't doing so well. I could use some help praying."

I rub my eyes, grab my new siddur, and head back to the ICU. A number of doctors are with Dov, trying different medications to lower his ICP. I decide to sit outside while watching Dov through the window. I open my siddur and begin to pray, but I cannot help but watch the ICP numbers as they rise, little by little, to dangerous levels. I focus on the Hebrew words I am saying; *perhaps*, I think, *if I pray harder, then the numbers will go down*. I concentrate hard, certain that my prayers will ward off the danger, but even with my focus on the words, I see the numbers are climbing higher.

Finally, I vow to shut out the ICP completely. I read Psalms with fervor, picturing myself standing before God, pleading my case. My eyes begin to water as I beg for His mercy. From somewhere in the depths of my soul, I find the words to address the Creator. *Dov's middle name is Matityahu, which means a gift from God. You gave us a gift, Lord. How can You take it back?*

I sit for hours with my tears and prayers. By the time I stop, I still don't know if my request will be granted, but somehow I feel, in my heart, that I have been heard.

Chapter 8
Friday morning, June 2, 2006

"I understand that there have been some issues with observing your holiday in the hospital," begins Eve, the social worker, who sits with us in the waiting room with a pen and pad of paper. "By the way," she asks, twirling her pen, "what holiday is it?"

"It's called Shavuot," explains Tzvi. "This is the holiday that commemorates when our people received the Ten Commandments."

"Shavuot. How do you spell that?"

I dictate the letters and she writes them down on her pad. "And the holiday is today?"

"It began last night, and it lasts two days. It doesn't end until tomorrow night after sundown," says Tzvi.

"Got it. And Mr. and Mrs. Klugerman—"

"Please, call us Yaffa and Tzvi."

"Yaffa," she writes, then stops. "How do you spell that?"

Needless to say, I have spent a significant part of my life telling people how to spell my name. I recite the letters to Eve, and then I tell her how to spell and pronounce Tzvi.

"Okay. Yaffa and Tzvi. How can we help you?"

"Well, for starters," I say, "we could really use some tissues."

Eve looks at me blankly. "Tissues?" she repeats.

"There are certain actions that we cannot do on our holidays," says Tzvi. "Ripping paper is one of those actions. So we can't tear toilet paper or paper towels in the bathrooms. We need tissues. And we need the boxes opened for us."

"That shouldn't be a problem at all. I can get you an entire carton of tissues."

"There's more," says Tzvi. "We're having trouble getting into the ICU to see our son."

"I've already told the staff about that," Eve says. "They know you can't ring the buzzer. You just need to ask someone to open the door for you and they'll do it."

Tzvi and I exchange glances. This won't be easy to explain. "No, it's...complicated," says Tzvi. "We can't ask anyone to do it for us. Our laws specifically prohibit us from asking someone to do these actions on our behalf. We can ask someone to do something for Dov without a problem, because his life is in danger, and the laws can be pushed aside for his sake. But not for us."

Eve puts her pen down. "Let me make sure I understand. Are you saying you can't ask someone to open the electric door for you?"

"That's exactly what I'm saying. You need to tell the staff to look out for us and to open the doors for us when they see us. We cannot ask them to do that."

Eve looks bewildered. "Look, here's an example," I interject. "Back in March, we wanted to buy tickets to a Billy Joel concert."

Tzvi nods. "Good example."

"But the tickets went on sale Saturday morning, which is our Sabbath, so we couldn't call or get on the Internet to buy tickets. We knew they would be sold out by Saturday night. I suggested that we ask someone who is not Jewish to buy us the tickets, but we realized we couldn't do that either, because we can't ask someone who doesn't observe the Sabbath to violate it for us."

"Billy Joel?" inquires Eve. "You like Billy Joel?"

"We *love* Billy Joel. We wanted to see him in concert for years."

"But you're telling me you didn't get to go because the tickets went on sale on Saturday."

"Well, not exactly," answers Tzvi, and he grins, remembering.

"So you got the tickets?"

"We got the tickets. But we did it in a unique way." And here I begin to laugh, thinking of that day.

"Well, now you have to tell me what happened!"

"We called my sister Sarah, who lives in Israel," I explain. "They're seven hours ahead of us. I gave her my credit card number and asked her to get on the Internet as soon as the Sabbath ended for her. That was about eleven thirty in the morning here. So she got us the tickets, and we went."

Eve starts to laugh. "So you got the tickets on the Sabbath after all."

"But it wasn't the Sabbath in Israel!"

"Okay. I get it. So the point is, you can't ask someone who is not Jewish to violate the holiday for you."

"Exactly."

Eve begins scribbling on her pad again. "Okay. Done. What else?"

"We would appreciate it if someone would bring us some water," I suggest.

"There's always water available in the ICU."

"Yes, there is, but from an electric machine. We can't operate it on the holiday, and we can't ask anyone to do it for us. And we're thirsty all the time."

"So," concludes Eve, "should the staff offer a cup of water to you when they see you?"

"Yes, that would be wonderful," I say. "That would be perfect. Even better, they could just fill a pitcher with ice water, so we have it for a while."

Eve is writing down PITCHER OF WATER on her pad. "What else?"

"I go to sleep in the lounge, but I can't turn off the light. I'd appreciate it if someone could just turn off the light if they see me lying down," I say.

LIGHTS, writes Eve.

"Also, here's another request, or really, it's just a tip: why aren't there any tissues in the chapel? Everyone who walks in there is crying. A box of tissues there would be a good idea."

Eve smiles. "Got it. And this holiday lasts for two days?"

I smile back. "Some years," I say, "it even lasts for three."

"Wow." Eve is incredulous. "How do you manage?"

Tzvi and I shrug. "The truth is that, at home, you just get used to it," says Tzvi. "You set a few timers, turn off your refrigerator light, and expect to do a lot of walking."

"Remarkable," says Eve.

"Look, actually we're lucky here," I say. "Imagine if the toilets were flushed automatically. Then we'd really have a problem."

"God," says Eve. "I wouldn't have thought about that." She closes her pad. "Wait right here. I'm going to take care of the tissues right now."

She returns a few minutes later, holding a carton filled with boxes of tissues. Carefully, she takes out each box and rips the top open. "Will this do?"

I have never been so happy to see a box of tissues in all my life. "This is perfect. Thank you."

"I will speak to the ICU staff and let them know about opening the door and offering you something to drink. It might take some time to get used to, but we will work it out. We want to help you as much as we can."

We are moved. "Thank you," says Tzvi.

"You're welcome. You know, I'm a Billy Joel fan, too."

Chapter 9
Friday afternoon, June 2, 2006

The doctors want to meet with us. Almost instinctively, I begin to shake with terror. Is this the end? Is Dov failing? I fold my arms and try to quiet my shivers as they walk into the waiting room and sit down with us.

"We're meeting with you," begins Dr. Santiago, "because we're recommending that we proceed with surgery for Dov."

"What kind of surgery?" asks Tzvi.

"It's called a craniectomy. Basically, what it means is that we will open up Dov's skull in order to allow room for his brain to expand without being squeezed."

"Right now, his intracranial pressure is very high," says Dr. Wein. "We've been trying to control it, but we haven't been successful. We feel that this surgery will give Dov his best chance."

"What happens if we don't consent to the surgery?" I ask.

"That's your choice," says Dr. Santiago. "We do not expect he will survive if the pressure is not relieved. I will be honest with you: I am not always in favor of this kind of surgery, because there's a good chance that it might save the patient, but he will be left in a vegetative state."

Here I shake even more violently. "Are you telling me that we have a choice between letting him die or letting him live in a vegetative state?"

"I didn't say that would *definitely* be the outcome if we operate. I said it could be. We just don't know. But we do think that this is the best option we have."

My voice is almost a whisper. "Do you think he could eventually recover?"

"We don't know," says Dr. Wein. "We just don't know. I've seen miracle children before, Mrs. Klugerman, and I can't rationally explain why some survive and some don't. We can only do our best."

Tzvi speaks now. "When would you do the surgery?"

"Immediately."

We are silent. "Can we have a few moments alone to discuss it?" asks Tzvi.

"Certainly."

The doctors file out and close the door. I am trembling so violently that my teeth chatter as I speak. This is unquestionably the worst decision I have ever had to make in my life, but I know what it has to be. "Tzvi, we have to do it. We have to go ahead with it, no matter what happens."

"I know."

"We have to know that we did everything we could to save him."

"I agree. But are you prepared for him to possibly live the rest of his life hooked up to a ventilator?"

I begin to cry. "Of course I'm not! I can't believe we're having this conversation! I just can't believe it! It's the hardest decision I've ever made!" I wipe my tears. "But we have to go ahead with this. There's no question that we have to do it."

"Okay." Tzvi takes a deep breath and suggests I do the same. "Are you ready to speak to the doctors?"

"Yes, let's call them in."

The doctors file in and we tell them to proceed. There is a consent form that we are required to sign.

"I'll need Eve to help me," says Tzvi. "Can you please call her?"

Eve joins us in the waiting room. "They need me to sign this form," Tzvi says. "I'll need your help. I'll sign my name because that's what is needed to help Dov, but that's all. Do you understand? It's still our holiday and I can't violate it."

Eve nods. Tzvi takes the pen in his hand and signs his name, and then gives the pen to Eve to fill in our address and the date. The doctors take the form and begin heading out to prepare for surgery.

As he exits, Dr. Santiago turns back to us. "I think you made the right decision."

We sit outside the operating room and wait. In other Jewish homes around the world, families are gathered around their tables, singing songs, giving Torah discourses, and enjoying delectable holiday foods. Tzvi, Dov, and I should be celebrating the holiday at home with the rest of the children, my parents, and my mother-in-law, as we had planned. Instead, we are sitting in an empty waiting room reciting Psalms. I clutch the siddur my mother gave me and repeat the same phrases over and over and over, asking, begging, imploring God to have mercy on our son. Have mercy on our family. Have mercy on us. After several hours, I cannot bring myself to pray anymore. I close my siddur and sit, lost in thought.

"Do you think he will get better?" I finally whisper.

Tzvi pauses. "We have to believe that he will."

"What is the point of hoping for something that might be impossible?"

"Because it just might be possible. Let's plan for Dov's recovery. I think we should have a *seudat hodaya*, to thank God and the community for their support. What do you think?"

"We'll have a big Kiddush at shul," I muse, "with kugels. Especially potato kugel. Dovie loves potato kugel."

"And lots of candy for the children."

"And we'll bring Dov along, of course. He'll be better by then. He'll be able to smile and thank everyone himself. And everyone will talk about his miraculous recovery, and how God listened to our prayers."

In this empty, lonely waiting room, we continue discussing our plans for Dov's recovery. We are dangling from a cliff by our fingertips, clutching at every tiny groove of hope we can find, convinced that if we hang on, we will eventually be rescued. In synagogues around the world, family and friends are praying with us, extending their hands down toward us. We sit alone, but in my mind, I see thousands reaching out to help us. *Hold on tight*, they seem to whisper.

Late in the day, Dr. Santiago emerges from the operating room. "The surgery was successful," he reports. "Dov's brain pressure improved tremendously. We are wheeling him into recovery."

"*Chasdei Hashem*," I murmur. *The kindness of God*.

We spend the second day of Shavuot in hopeful spirits. In the early afternoon, my sister Sarah calls from Israel, where night has fallen and the holiday has ended. She speaks to the nurse, who cannot quite understand why we refuse to come to the phone but still want to hear what Sarah has to say.

"It's my sister," I explain. "Tell her that they operated on Dov, and that he's stable, thank God."

The nurse relays the message and then, listening to Sarah some more, she frowns, looking confused.

"What did she say?" Tzvi asks.

"I don't understand," says the nurse. "She says...Billy Joel tickets?"

Tzvi and I burst out laughing. In between gasps, I respond. "Tell her...tell her not this time, but thanks anyway."

Later in the day, Tzvi's friend and colleague, Rabbi Shmuel Feld, walks several miles from his home to visit us in the hospital. Soon afterwards, a group of Yeshiva students do the same. Unable to drive because of the holiday, they have trekked nearly ten miles in the Washington DC heat without being able to carry water bottles. Fortunately, the nurses now know to provide us with pitchers of ice water, which we offer to them. We also offer them a generous assortment of cakes, which Bikur Cholim provided for me and Tzvi, but was far more than the two of us could have ever eaten.

"This is delicious," says one student as he downs a chunk of cake. "Did you make this?"

"I didn't make anything," I respond.

There are ten men all together, enough for a *minyan*—a quorum needed for public prayer. Tzvi asks the doctors if they can pray their afternoon and evening prayers in Dov's room, and the request is granted. Once again, I watch the surreal scene. From within Dov's room, the boys and men chant our ancient prayers together, while I hope their words bring God's mercy. In the center of the room lies Dov, eyes closed, totally still, his head bandaged in swathes of cloth that look like a white turban, which my father later says is reminiscent of the one that was worn by the High Priest in the Holy Temple in Jerusalem.

Can Dov hear them pray? I hope so.

I gaze at my husband. We've been married for sixteen happy years. How did we wind up here?

Chapter 10
August 1988

M y oldest brother Yitzie was about to get married, and the *aufruf* was scheduled to take place at my parents' house in Margate, New Jersey. At twenty-one years old, he was the first of my eight siblings to get engaged, to move on to this new stage and, to me, there was something completely incomprehensible about it. It was an indication that we were all starting to grow up. One day, we might *all* actually become adults.

I was twenty at the time, and attending Stern College in Manhattan, so I asked Yitzie if anyone else was going from New York who could give me a lift.

"Sure," he said. "Call Tzvi."

Tzvi Klugerman and Yitzie had been close friends for years, ever since they discovered that their rooms were next door to each other at Yeshiva University's Rubin dorm. Tzvi was from Brooklyn, and I had heard a lot about him, but had only met him briefly once, when he came to visit Stern. I felt a bit strange reaching out to someone I barely knew, but I decided to give him a call anyway, and he told me to meet him in Brooklyn on Friday.

I took the subway to the Avenue U station in Brooklyn, where Tzvi picked me up in his car and brought me to his parents' house on Batchelder Street. Two of Yitzie's friends, David Rosenfeld and Ron Ostroff, were joining us; they were coming for the *aufruf* as well.

"Would you like some orange juice?" asked Tzvi's mother. "Or something to eat?"

"No thanks," I said, "I'm fine."

"Nothing at all? Are you sure?"

"Ma, leave her alone," Tzvi said. "We are just about ready to leave anyway."

"Do you want to take some food for the road?" his mother asked.

"Ma, she's *fine*. We have enough snacks."

"Yaffa, you know of any good girls for my son? He really needs to find a wife."

"I'll keep that in mind," I replied with a smile. Tzvi was twenty-three years old and still a student at YU, so he was not quite an old bachelor yet, although perhaps his mother thought differently.

Tzvi closed his eyes and shook his head. "Ma, enough. Guys, let's get out of here."

We settled ourselves in the car, a black Delta 88. I was in the front with Tzvi, while Ron and David sat in the back. The trip to Margate generally took about two and a half hours, but maybe forty-five minutes had passed before we noticed a light glowing on the dashboard.

"Oh no, she's hot," said Tzvi.

"She? Who is she?" I asked.

"My car. She's overheating. I have to pull over."

"Your car is a *she*?"

"Cars are always shes."

We stopped on the side of the highway, and Tzvi popped the hood and stared inside.

"No coolant," he said. "There must be a leak."

"So, what do we do?" said Ron.

It was just a few hours until Shabbat. If we returned to Brooklyn to switch cars, we would never make it to Margate on time. And that was assuming we even *had* another car to switch to—which we didn't.

"We're going to limp her to Margate," Tzvi decided. "We'll keep the heat on and the windows open to keep her from overheating. And I'll just keep stopping the car and adding coolant."

It admittedly seemed counterintuitive to me that the way to keep the car from overheating was by cranking up the heat, but that's how we spent the next four hours driving to Margate. Even with the windows open, the heat was suffocating; with the hot air blowing through the car, I felt like I was in a giant hair dryer. By the third time we had to stop to add coolant, I got out of the car just to escape the stickiness of the seat. I stood on the side of the road, watching Tzvi pour coolant into his car.

He was wearing denim shorts and a plaid button-down shirt, now dampened with sweat. Under his yarmulke was a mess of chestnut curls, and his face was framed with a trim beard. *He's cute*, I thought.

"All done," he said.

As I got back into the car, he came around to shut my door for me. I looked out the window to thank him and, just for a second, our eyes met and held.

We arrived in Margate in the nick of time, just before Shabbat. I spent the weekend enjoying being with my family. Throughout the Shabbat, and later, at the wedding on Sunday afternoon in Philadelphia, Tzvi and I barely exchanged a word although, more than once, I caught him looking at me.

After the wedding, we headed back to New York, only this time with five people in the car. Again, I sat up front with Tzvi. Three passengers were squashed into the back seat. The car was still overheating and, every few miles, we stopped to let it cool down. Pretty soon the car reeked of sweat.

Between the heavy Labor Day weekend traffic and the overheating car, it took six hours to get back to New York. Arriving at Stern, I stumbled out of the car, said thank you to Tzvi and headed up to the dorm. It had been an extremely long day, and all I could think about was taking a nice, long shower.

The next day I received a message from Tzvi on my answering machine. Yitzie and Ruthie were having *sheva brachot* in New Jersey; would I like a ride?

I called him. "Is your car fixed?"

"No, but I want to go anyway. I'm going to rent a car. Do you want to come?"

Indeed, I did.

He picked me up from the dorm and this time, we were dressed to party. I was wearing a striped skirt and matching top that I had borrowed from my roommate, and Tzvi liked it immediately.

"You look good in that," he said.

"Thanks." I could feel myself glowing.

The car couldn't have been more than a year old and the air conditioning, I noticed, worked perfectly, just as it ought. Tzvi and I talked about Yitzie and his wife Ruthie, about college, and about the fact, strange to us, that I had eight siblings, while he was an only child. The banter was easy and free flowing. After spending so many hours together in an overheated car, we talked like old friends.

The *sheva brachot* was a barbeque, so we sat outdoors on folding chairs at folding tables. I sat next to Pnina, another English major from my college. We exchanged small talk, and then halfway through the meal, I heard a voice.

"Hey Pnina," said Tzvi. "Can you switch places with me for a few minutes?"

The next thing I knew, Tzvi had taken the place next to me. I was a little flabbergasted. Most guys I knew would not be that forward. It took nerve for someone to make a move so openly. It was clear that he liked me, and everyone there could see it. I found myself liking it, and found myself liking this man who so obviously liked me.

On the way home, Tzvi agreed to take Steve Toplan, my new sister-in-law's brother, back to Yeshiva University in Washington

Heights. I was surprised when Tzvi made Washington Heights his first stop, rather than Midtown, where he would let me off.

"I have something to take care of in Manhattan," Tzvi explained to Steve.

I don't know if Steve believed this, but he said his thanks and left. Tzvi and I remained in the car, sitting in the front seat, as we seemed to have been doing for quite some time now. I gazed at the lights of Manhattan as we sped by in our swank car rental. Our studies had just started, but it was still summer in the city. My dorm was right down the block from the Empire State Building, and as we got close to it, Tzvi turned to me.

"So," he said, "seeing anyone?"

I looked at him, and my heart started to beat fast. "Um. Not really."

"Accepting applications?"

I laughed. "Maybe."

"Well," he said, "I'm applying."

I could barely hold back my smile.

"Look," he said, "I think we get along great. I'd like to get to know you better. What do you say?"

With that, I stopped trying to hold back my smile. I liked this guy. I wanted to get to know him better, too. "Yes," I answered.

Many years later, Tzvi would tell me he had rented the car specifically to get the chance to take me out. It was the most expensive "date" he had ever planned. "But it was worth it," he said. "It was the best investment I ever made."

Chapter 11
Saturday night, June 3, 2006

The holiday is over. Dov's vital signs appear stable, and it's time for me to go to the mikvah. Immersing myself regularly is as basic to me as eating kosher or keeping Shabbat: When it's time to go, I just do it. I have walked miles on Shabbat to immerse in a mikvah, I have excused myself from tables full of guests—without explanation—to arrive at the mikvah on time. During summers when I've worked at camp, I have even plunged into a freezing lake. Yet tonight, I am faced with obstacles I have never anticipated. I do not wish to leave the hospital for a long time, and although the closest mikvah is in DC, I haven't made arrangements for an attendant to meet me, and I have no idea how to get there. I call our friend, Sharon Freundel, who is in charge of the DC mikvah, and tell her my predicament.

"Look," she says, "your son is in the ICU, and you should be at his side. You and your husband are going to be staying in the hospital. There is no reason for you to be going tonight."

I am feeling increasingly desperate. "This is the lowest point of my life," I say. "I want to be able to hold my husband's hand. Do you understand? *I want to hold Tzvi's hand.*"

Sharon is silent. "Well," she finally says, "that's something else entirely. Let's try to work something out."

The directions to the mikvah are complicated, so Sharon suggests I simply call a taxi to deliver me there directly. I say goodbye to Tzvi and wait downstairs in the parking lot, but the taxi doesn't arrive. Fifteen minutes later, I call again, but the dispatcher can't tell me when the car is expected. I am determined to wait, but I become discouraged when I see several rabbis and their wives coming to visit Dov. They spot me immediately, and I can read the confusion in their eyes: *What exactly is Mrs. Klugerman doing in the parking lot when her son is critically injured in the ICU?* I mumble something incoherently about needing to run an errand, and they tell me they are all praying for Dov's speedy recovery.

I wait some more, but after a half hour passes and a fifth rabbinical couple eyes me questioningly, my determination wanes. Feeling utterly defeated, I call Sharon and explain the situation.

"Come tomorrow morning," she suggests, "before all your visitors arrive. As you know, we usually go to mikvah at night, but this is a special situation, and it's not forbidden to go during the day. I'll pick you up at nine thirty."

I thank her and return to the ICU, feeling dejected but hopeful about the next day. When Sharon arrives in the morning, I am grateful to leave the walls of the hospital for a little while. Sharon is a former ICU nurse, and she and I talk about Dov's condition.

"Tell me the truth," I say, "is it possible for Dov to recover?"

"It's possible. The brain can heal. But you're in for the long haul."

The long haul, I think. *I can deal with that.*

She escorts me to the mikvah, a beautiful, sparkling-clean new facility that even has a Jacuzzi in the bathtub. Unfortunately, time is of the essence, and Sharon recommends that instead of bathing, as is usually required, I take a thorough shower. I agree; I want to get back to the hospital as quickly as possible. As soon as she closes the door, I swiftly disrobe and begin the familiar mikvah preparations I have performed since I was a bride. I have not worn makeup in days, but still I remove whatever traces remain on my face. I brush and floss my teeth, clean my ears, blow my nose, and shower thoroughly. And then I look at my nails, and I realize that the preparation will be more time-consuming than I had realized.

Ten days earlier, I had treated myself to a professional manicure and pedicure—the first I'd ever had—in honor of my brother Akiva's wedding. In order to immerse in the mikvah, all traces of nail polish must be removed. As I sit in the bathroom looking at my painted nails, I remember that glorious wedding day: Our boys and Tzvi looking dapper in their tuxedos, Sarit beautiful in a gown we had made for her—a lavender two-piece which she designed on her own. I had worn a purple gown that fit and flattered me perfectly. Both of our gowns displayed matching fabric flowers fastened to the front. On the morning of the wedding, I had arrived at the nail salon clutching that fabric flower from my gown. I chose a shade of nail polish to match, and then I sat, in pampered luxury, as the attendant washed my hands and feet, filed my nails, and applied base coat, polish, and top coat. When it was finished, I felt like royalty. And later, when our family posed for a picture, I glanced around at my loved ones with joy, breathing in the heady scent of the purple and lavender flowers that Sarit and I clutched. At that moment in time, everything had been absolutely perfect.

And now I sit in the bathroom next the mikvah furiously wiping my nails with nail polish remover, trying to remove the last traces of that perfect day, but the polish stubbornly clings to my nails, refusing to let go, until I have to stifle the insane urge to rip them out entirely. *Oh, God!* I think desperately. *What have You done to me?* I grip the cotton balls doused in acetone and I rub my nails ferociously, back and forth, over and over, slowly removing the layers of polish. Back and forth, again and again, on each nail, until the cotton balls seem to be chanting a refrain: *"It is over, over, over,"* they whisper. *"Your life is over, over, over."*

I begin to weep, my tears splashing on the nails that had once been so perfectly manicured. I ache for the innocence of that glorious wedding day, when my worst problem was worrying about creasing my gown, or the boys spilling soda on their tuxedos, fearing that Noam wouldn't smile for the picture, and hoping that Tzvi's tie would match!

Oh God! To have a day when I didn't know terror and pain as I do today!

My nails clipped and bare, my hair wet and combed, my makeup removed, I check myself in the mirror, wipe my eyes, and call Sharon to escort me to the mikvah. As I enter the warm waters, I close my eyes, and say a silent prayer for what I want most:

Please, God, I implore, *heal my son. Heal Dov.*

Chapter 12
Sunday afternoon, June 4, 2006

We have received what feels like well over a hundred visitors since the morning. Tzvi and I appreciate the visits, but we are exhausted. Dov appears to be stable at the moment, and so we tell the medical staff that we want to run home to change our clothes and spend time with our kids. We haven't been home in three days. My mother-in-law agrees to stay with Dov in the meantime, and we grab our suitcases and leave.

Earlier that day, my parents drove our children to the hospital so that they could visit Dov for the first time since his accident. Together, we sat in Dov's room, where he lay unconscious, hooked up to a machine that was helping him breathe. He was a shadow of the big brother they knew, the brother they both loved and hated—the boy who could both love them to pieces and drive them insane. Neither Tzvi nor I could reassure them that all would be well, although we desperately wanted to.

When we arrive home, we find a stack of letters waiting for us on our dining room table. I glance, almost unseeing, at the usual bills and circulars, and then my eyes come to rest on a letter from the Jewish Federation of Greater Washington. I tear open the envelope and read:

Dear Rabbi and Mrs. Klugerman,
    All of us at the Federation are saddened to hear about the tragedy that has struck your family this week.

I hope that you can draw comfort and strength from the community that you have helped to make a better and stronger one through your personal and professional endeavors. Please know that I, and the Jewish Federation, are here to support you in any way that you need.

Your son is in my thoughts and prayers.

A *tragedy*. It's the first time I've heard Dov's accident referred to in this way. Is that what this is? Are these tragic circumstances? All along, we have been tending to Dov's care, but this is the first time I step back and see the situation from this perspective. Dov's accident is a tragedy. We are part of a tragedy.

It is all too much to absorb.

We hug our children, unload our dirty laundry, gather fresh clothes. I am surprised to find the house so tidy after a two-day holiday, followed by a Sunday. I expected to find shoes strewn about, coats on the floor, and dishes in the sink. "A cleaning lady came to take care of everything," explains Sarit. "I don't know who she was." It is one of the many kindnesses that people have begun quietly extending to us.

Avichai wants us to read him a book. Tzvi acquiesces, and the two of them sit down on our living room sofa. I glance through our emails; there are dozens. We don't have enough time to go through them all.

We are in the car, about to leave, when I remember a suggestion from the nurses and I run back into the house to grab two CDs that Dovie likes. Perhaps, I think, he'd like to hear these.

As we pull out of our driveway and pass his school, I turn my head away.

That night, as Tzvi is busy elsewhere, I sit in Dov's hospital room and listen to Israeli singer Idan Raichel's song, *Mima'amakim*, being played on a CD player the nurses have set up next to his bed. It's a love song, but the title is reminiscent of a well-known psalm I have recited over and over again during the past few days:

Mima'amakim kiraticha Hashem
From the depths, I call to You, Lord

Ladies and gentlemen, welcome to the depths.

The monitor flashes Dov's vital signs, the ventilator pumps oxygen into him, the IV drips fluids into his veins. These are the surreal metronomes of the ICU, ticking along with the haunting rhythm of Idan Raichel.

Last week, this song was playing in my car as I took Dov to his tutor, and he demanded that I play it again. It is one of his favorites.

Without warning, my tears begin to fall, and I find myself sobbing, gasping for air, my head in my hands, my shoulders heaving, listening to Idan Raichel crooning in the background.

Last week!

Last week Dov was healthy; today he lies in intensive care. Last week he could breathe by himself; today he is hooked up to a ventilator. Last week he had his entire life in front of him. Today, his life hangs by a thread. Last week, we were a normal family. Today, we are part of a tragedy.

From the depths, I call to you, Lord!

I had cried before, but not like this. A few tears here and there, perhaps the occasional sob, but not this wheezing, gasping, hysterical, uncontrollable weeping that hasn't overtaken me since I was a child, when a scratch on the knee felt like a catastrophe. Perhaps it takes a catastrophe to summon this type of crying. The notes of the song pierce my soul until I feel as if my emotions have been not just released, but splattered all over the room. How many other parents' tears have these walls seen?

From somewhere beyond the depths, I feel a hand on my shoulder. It is Jo, the nurse who has been lovingly tending to Dov, coming to calm me down.

"You've been very brave," she says, "and Dov is counting on you."

I close my eyes, nod my head, and reach for a tissue. There is no point in crying. If I give in to despair, I can't fight for Dov. I inhale, swallow my sobs, and force myself to focus on her words.

"Are you okay?"

I nod, not yet ready to speak.

In the background, I hear the last notes of Idan Raichel's song.

SPIRITUAL HEALING | 75

Chapter 13
Spiritual Healing

Tzvi has decided that he is going to write a book when this is over, and the title is going to be: *There Are No Litvaks in the ICU.* In his heart, Tzvi has always fancied himself a *Litvak*—Jews of Lithuanian background and leanings who have a reputation for no-nonsense, rational, and intellectual observance. Who would have thought that practical, realistic Rabbi Klugerman, who pooh-poohs lucky red strings, *segulahs*, good-luck amulets, and spiritual reawakenings, would go along with the many and varied kabbalistic ideas that have been offered and attempted to help heal Dov?

The spiritual therapies begin as soon as Shavuot ends. First, a friend recommends someone who claims to heal by touch, and without a second thought, we agree to allow her to check Dov. Then the *segulahs* begin to arrive: holy water from the renowned late rabbi Baba Sali, known for its healing powers, as well as a dollar bill blessed by the late Lubavitcher Rebbe.

The religious healing activity only intensifies after the doctors have informed us of the extent of Dov's dire circumstances. At one point, community members go to great lengths to transport a purportedly therapeutic bottle of wine, blessed by the great Rabbi Kanievsky in Israel, to the United States. Via a flurry of emails and phone calls, they find a former student of Tzvi's traveling from Israel to DC who agrees to escort the wine. The student is cautioned not to allow anyone else to touch the container, and so he sits, throughout the eleven-hour flight, learning Talmud in merit of Dov's recovery, guarding the precious wine that is contained in a plastic bottle placed in a shoe box. Upon arriving in Washington, the former student meets his father, who takes the wine directly to Children's Hospital and places it in Tzvi's hands. Included in the package are sugar candies from Rabbi Kanievsky's wife, which are also reputed to possess healing qualities.

We are instructed to wet Dov's lips with the wine, and to give him the candies when—not if—he regains consciousness. My father and I stand next to Dov as Tzvi carefully brushes drops of the blessed wine on Dov's lips. We watch the monitors, particularly the one that indicates the dropping oxygen level in Dov's brain, and wait for a miracle to occur.

My mother hears of a bizarre mystical cure: Gather water from seven ocean waves, pour it on Dov's hands, and then wash the floor with it. The challenge? Dov is hospitalized in Washington, DC, which is nowhere near an ocean. My mother is not deterred; she reaches out to my sister Adina in Miami Beach.

"This is going to sound a little crazy," my mother tells her. "But I need you to gather some waves for Dovie."

My sister is ready and willing. "If you told me that it would help to run naked down my street waving chickens, I would do that too," she says.

So my extremely pregnant sister takes a large plastic container to the beach and wades into the ocean, trying to "catch" pieces of seven waves. She almost succeeds, but an unexpected current literally knocks her off her feet. As she falls, she loses her grip on the plastic container, which is carried out to sea. Later, she will say that it felt like someone had just pushed her over.

When she tells her husband Avi what happened, he offers to try. He is successful. He carefully packages the container which holds the precious ocean water and sends it next-day air. My mother tracks the package closely, but just as it is about to be delivered, it disappears from her computer screen. She tries to locate it, and is finally told that the package was destroyed.

"Ema," says Adina, "I don't think Dovie was meant to receive those waves."

None of the mystical remedies has any effect on Dov's condition, but what we discover is that illness has the power to unite people. A person in crisis reaches out blindly for support and welcomes any that is offered. It makes no difference where that support comes from or how outlandish it may be; great strength is found from simply knowing that people care.

We appreciate prayers for Dov from anyone and everyone. One doctor says he is using his rosary beads for Dov, and we are touched. A secular humanistic rabbi—a denomination of Judaism that does not espouse belief in God—tells us he is praying for Dov. Although we wonder privately who, exactly, the rabbi is praying to, we appreciate his concern. Our neighbor, a Greek Orthodox Christian, informs my mother that Dov is in their prayers. "We all have one God," she explains simply.

Late one night, a man approaches Tzvi, who is outside Dov's room in the ICU, whispering prayers. "Can you pray for my son, too?" asks the man.

"Of course," Tzvi replies. "What's his name?"

"Christopher."

"And what's his mother's name?"

"Mary."

Without a second thought, Tzvi begins to pray for a complete recovery for Christopher, son of Mary.

We become acquainted with another ICU family: A father and grandfather, keeping vigil over a child who has survived a car accident. Another child, they tell us, is dead. The mother is being treated in the hospital next door. We sit together and discuss our horror stories. We sympathize with each other, and we know that the sympathy is genuine.

As the hours wear on, I receive text messages describing efforts to pray for Dov. Adina tells me that the entire school where she teaches in Florida has just recited from the book of Psalms for Dov. Yitzie shares that several thousand people in

Lakewood, New Jersey, have included Dov in their prayers. Sarah tells me that Dov's name has been circulated throughout Israel, and hundreds are praying for him. We receive hundreds of get-well cards from students within our community. Both the Yeshiva and Dov's old school, MJBHA, send cassette tapes filled with get-well wishes from Dov's classmates to be played for him.

While I walk around the ICU clutching a blanket around my shoulders to quiet my shivers of terror, an enormous blanket of love and support is being spread over all our family by our friends and relatives, and even people we've never met.

Our neighbor Judy is at the epicenter of these efforts. While Tzvi and I are at the hospital with Dov, she and a sizable committee of women have been running our household. When she comes to visit us in the hospital, she shows me a list of people who have volunteered to help with meals, carpooling, laundry, and an endless number of other jobs. There are over two hundred names listed.

"Who *are* all these people?" I ask Judy. Then another thought comes to me. "I should have invited them to Dov's bar mitzvah." The somber atmosphere is momentarily forgotten in our laughter.

"You wouldn't believe it, Yaffa," she says. "People are just clamoring to help. I can barely keep them from breaking down the door."

"But why? I mean, it's wonderful, and very appreciated, but why do they care so much?"

Judy pauses to gather her thoughts. "I think you're much more loved than you realize."

I am in complete disbelief. "I don't know how I can possibly thank them all enough."

"They aren't looking for thanks. They just want to help you in whatever way they can."

Yitzie is in touch with us regularly about Dov's condition and circulates updates to hundreds of people throughout the world. His emails reach friends and acquaintances we haven't seen or heard from in decades, but who nevertheless want to help.

Yitzie and Sarah announce plans to coordinate a massive and ongoing prayer effort: They will be enlisting people to pray for at least a half hour a day for Dov, in order to have a minimum of ten people praying for him continually at all hours of the day. People across the globe sign up, selecting their time slots on the list, until nearly four hundred men and women have agreed to devote at least thirty minutes of their day to praying for Dov's recovery.

Every day, volunteers arrive at the hospital to deliver food and drinks, not just to us, but to all the friends and family who are staying with us. Our dear friend, Fran Kritz, works tirelessly with Bikur Cholim to make sure that everyone at the hospital is well-fed. There is so much food, in fact, that we wind up giving some to families of other patients who, like us, are standing vigil in the hospital day and night. On one memorable day, Bikur Cholim even arranges to bring pizza for the entire ICU staff.

Every day, I sit with my checkbook, pen in hand, and send out hundreds of dollars to worthy organizations and charities, not at all certain how we will cover all that we are promising to give. But our tradition says that *tzedakah* has the power to save one from death, and that belief is enough to prod me to keep doling out more. That, and my memories of Dov's bar mitzvah.

Less than two hours before our big Shabbat had been about to begin, my niece had run through our glass patio door, smashing it to bits and leaving her face cut and bloodied. Our house, packed with relatives and friends who had arrived to celebrate with us, became a scene of chaos as we made frantic arrangements for a plastic surgeon to attend to my niece immediately, so she could get stitches before Shabbat began. As we sent our niece and her family to the hospital, and the rest of our guests to their hosts, Tzvi and I had knelt down on the carpet to gather up the shards of glass.

Outside, sheets of rain cascaded from the sky. Then Yitzie announced that his car wouldn't start, and he needed to find

a mechanic immediately. The phone rang, and it was the pho-
tographer waiting for us at the synagogue, telling us that there
was no power in the building.

This can't be a coincidence, I thought. *All these things going
wrong at once; it must be a sign.* I've neglected something. I ran
through everything we had done to prepare for Dov's bar mitzvah. We had spent more money than we ever had, since buying
our house. But had we given enough *tzedakah*? I realized that
in the hustle and bustle of our preparations, we had neglected
this essential mitzvah.

Despite not knowing how we would cover it, I sat down
at the kitchen table and wrote a significant check to a worth-
while cause. I placed it in an envelope and sealed it. *And now,*
I whispered, *I want all these problems to go away.*

Ten minutes later, the power was back on at the shul, Yitzie
called to say that his car had started again, and my brother Ari
called from the hospital to tell me that the plastic surgeon had
stitched up my niece in record time, and they would be back
in time for pictures.

After Shabbat, my father handed me a check. "I figured
you could use some help," he said with a wink. I looked at the
sum, which more than covered what I had pledged to *tzedakah*
the day before.

Later, we received a call from my brother Akiva who wasn't
able to come for the bar mitzvah because he was serving as an
Israel Defense Forces soldier in the Gaza Strip. There had been a
bombing at his base the night before, he told us, but he was okay.

I told Akiva about the check I had written the day before.
"Do you think it helped you?"

"Yaffa," he responded, "I have no doubt that it did."

Now, as I sit in the hospital nearly two years later, I hope
with all my heart that somehow, this *tzedakah* will help Dov.
At one point, I realize with dismay that my stock of envelopes
has been totally depleted. With urgency in my voice, I ask a
nurse if she can somehow locate some for me. She appears

confused; later I realize that, of all the requests a parent might make, envelopes wouldn't be one she would expect. Still, she manages to bring me some, and I thank her profusely as I insert more checks and affix stamps.

Tzvi and I decide to enlist our friends to give *tzedakah* too. Together, we write the following email:

> *Teshuva, tefilla, tzedakah ma'avirin et ro'a hagezeira.* Prayer, repentance and charity avert the evil decree. We have seen the effects of your prayers, and we are grateful. Our family is currently involved in *teshuva*. As Dov approaches his fifteenth birthday, we would ask everyone to give fifteen (the numerical equivalent of God's name) of any denomination—pennies, dollars, shekels—to any *tzedaka*, in the merit of the complete recovery of Dov Matityahu. Thank you so much.

We hope that the number fifteen will be easy to give quickly; it's simpler to give a ten and a five than, say, the traditional amount of eighteen (or multiples of eighteen), which equals the equivalent of the word "life," but requires singles.

The message is sent via email. Later, we will find out that hundreds of people responded to our plea, many whom we had never even met.

And we continue to think: what more can we do? What else can be done to save Dov?

Chapter 14
Monday morning, June 5, 2006

The doctors want to meet with us. The waiting room is in use, so this time we meet in an examining room. My legs are shaking. I clutch Tzvi's hand tightly.

"Mr. and Mrs. Klugerman, as you know, we've been monitoring Dov constantly, and we operated on him on Friday in an effort to relieve the swelling in his brain," begins Dr. Santiago. "Initially, as you know, we were hopeful. Unfortunately, we are not so optimistic now. Dov's CAT scan shows worsening swelling of the upper part of his brain and injury to the brainstem."

It was 2:00 am on May 22, 1998, and I was giving birth to Noam. I was standing on the driveway outside our house, waiting for Tzvi to get back from fetching our neighbor, Ginger Pinchot, to watch our children. My membranes had ruptured, and I was doubled over with debilitating contractions. As I saw my husband return, all of a sudden, I felt the baby's head crowning.

"TZVI!" I screamed. "The baby's coming! The baby's coming!"

"Get into the car!" he commanded. "I'll get you to the hospital in five minutes."

I shook my head. "We don't have five minutes! This baby is being born now!"

Ginger was following him. "Tzvi," she called, "call an ambulance. There isn't time. There's a nurse who lives on this block. I'll go find her."

"I examined Dov this morning," says Dr. Wein. "He showed no signs of brain activity whatsoever."

Tzvi swallows hard. "What did the EEG show?"

"We can't do an EEG at this point. The pentobarbital—the drug which we gave him to induce the coma—is still in his system, and it hinders the outcome of the EEG."

"Well," says Tzvi, "then we'll have to wait until the pentobarbital is out of his system so we can do the EEG properly. I'm not convinced it's over yet."

Tzvi gripped my arm and led me inside. I tried hard to breathe, tried hard to stay calm, but I had never been so frightened in all my life. Tzvi, who once volunteered for Magen David Adom in Israel, guided me down to the floor in our living room and examined me.

"I have to push! Tzvi! I have to push! I can't take it!"

Oh, God, the pressure! Intense, merciless, earth-splitting pressure. I am being torn in half. I am going to die.

"Okay. Okay. Breathe. Push. Now wait, stop pushing!"

Without me realizing it, he removed the umbilical cord from around the neck of the baby.

"Mr. Klugerman, I'm not hopeful. As you know, his blood pressure dropped dangerously low, and we had to administer drugs in order to keep his heart beating."

"Perhaps, once his brain begins to heal, the blood pressure will stabilize."

"Mr. Klugerman, I examined Dov today. All the signs show that his body is shutting down."

"I don't believe it. There's still hope."

"Okay. Go ahead and push!"

And with one quick, effective push, baby Noam slithered out, crying heartily, to be caught by his father.

"Ginger!" Tzvi yelled. "I need a towel!"

Ginger had just then arrived with the nurse. Their faces reflected their shock. I tried to imagine how we must have looked: Rabbi Klugerman, triumphantly clutching a naked, crying newborn still attached to its umbilical cord, with me lying stretched out on our amniotic fluid-stained living room carpet.

"I can't believe this," I said. "I cannot believe I just gave birth in my living room."

"You are lucky to have such a resourceful husband," said Ginger.

When we spent summers at camp, Tzvi trained lifeguards to save lives. At work, Tzvi rescued kids who were failing in school. At home, he delivered babies. There wasn't a problem that Tzvi couldn't solve.

Until now.

"Mr. Klugerman, there's acid in his blood. That means that his kidneys are no longer functioning properly."

Upon hearing this, my husband, the same dauntless man who once delivered our child unassisted, bows his head and begins to weep. I sit by his side, hollow, silent, and powerless.

"Mr. Klugerman, I cannot tell you for sure what the outcome is going to be, but it doesn't look good. His pupils are dilated. Mr. Klugerman, I'm sorry to have to tell you this, but I've seen those eyes before. *I've seen those eyes before.*"

I think of the hundreds of people who are praying for Dov right now. I think of my parents and my mother-in-law, waiting expectantly outside, hoping to hear good news. I think of our plans to set up a web page for Dov to update people about his condition. Next to me, Tzvi weeps. And suddenly, I feel the last vestiges of our hopes fading.

"What will we tell our parents?" I whisper. "What will we tell our children and friends? What do we say?"

Dr. Wein pauses. "If you like, I can write up a statement for you to share. It will explain everything. And that way you won't have to think about the words."

"That would be helpful."

"I'll go work on it right now," he says as he leaves the room.

"There's something else," says Dr. Santiago. "At this point, we've reached the stage where we are no longer doing something *for* Dov if we have to restart his heart again. Instead, we are doing something *to* him. We have a checklist of medical interventions we use in situations like this, when a patient is failing. You can decide not to use any of them, or some of them, or all of them. It's up to you. But it's time to start thinking about these things. So I am going to give you this checklist, and you let us know what you'd like us to do. We'll do whatever we can to help you, no matter what you decide."

He hands me the paper. Tzvi, still weeping, nods. "We'll think it over carefully," he says.

A few minutes later, Dr. Wein returns with a typed statement. It reads:

> As most of you know, Dov was hit by a car late last week. His initial injuries included a severe injury to the base of his brain, called the brainstem. This area of the brain is responsible for wakefulness, breathing, and is an important connection for the rest of his brain to communicate with his body. The doctors were very pessimistic about his recovery in the initial 12 hours because this injury is usually fatal. However, Dov showed some signs of recovery of function the first night he was in the hospital, and he seemed to be responding to the therapies provided him. On last Friday, the pressure in Dov's brain became life-threatening. Under the advice of the doctors, we agreed to have him undergo a brain

surgery to relieve the pressure. He was also given medication to limit the pressure in his brain and allow the best chance for recovery.

Over the weekend, while the pressure remained relatively stable, other complications began to occur. Now, on Monday, he is having an increasing problem with his lungs. He has had a harder and harder time getting oxygen from the ventilator into his lungs. He has had a harder time getting rid of acid from his blood, a function that his lungs and kidneys should be handling better. And most importantly, he had a CAT scan of his brain that showed worsening swelling of the upper part of his brain along with continued injury to the brainstem.

In the next 48 hours, the doctors are going to administer several tests that will help us learn if Dov's brain is viable. It is also possible that Dov's physical condition may lead to a state where the doctors cannot keep his heart going. Again, we and the doctors will do everything possible to save Dov's life. But it might be out of both the doctors' and our hands.

Tzvi clicks his pen and adds a final sentence to the statement:

And the true refuah is all in God's hands.

Chapter 15
Tuesday, June 6, 2006, 5:30 am

Bikur Cholim has arranged for us to stay in a hotel room nearby, but Tzvi insists on spending the night in the hospital with Dov. Exhausted, I opt to sleep in the hotel room, but I get up early to shower and return to the ICU in time for Tzvi to head to morning prayers. To my horror, when I turn on the faucet in the bathroom I find that there is no hot water, and I wind up taking an ice-cold shower. I emerge, dripping and shivering, only this time from cold rather than fear. As I towel off, I hear the shrill buzz of the telephone.

"Hello?"

"Yaffa, you need to get down here. Get down here now." Tzvi's voice is marked by fatigue and urgency.

"What's happening?"

"Dov's blood pressure dropped. He's failing. The doctors are working on him right now. I need to call home to tell Sarit not to go on the New York trip."

I hang up quickly and throw on my clothes, and then bolt out of the room. *Dammit, dammit, dammit! I should have spent the night in the waiting room!*

There's supposed to be a shuttle to the hospital, but the guard has no idea when it will arrive. I burst out of the lobby and begin to run. Heart pounding, chest heaving, breath coming in gasps, I arrive at the ICU in ten minutes. Out of the corner of my eye, I see friends who have come to deliver us breakfast. They try to greet me, but I barely nod as I run inside.

"They brought him back," Tzvi tells me, gripping my shoulders as I rush in. "He's still alive."

Dov is surrounded by doctors and nurses. I note with horror that the oxygen-level indicator now points to zero on both sides of his brain. But he has a pulse.

"It was very sudden," says Tzvi. "His blood pressure just dropped. They had to give him some heavy-duty drugs to save him."

I am still gasping. Is it because of the run or because of fear? Or both?

Later, we will hear how Sarit, who had been counting down the days to her eighth grade New York trip, had spent hours packing her suitcase the night before. That morning, she dressed quickly and stood by the door, her suitcase by her side, anxiously waiting to be picked up by her friend to meet the bus to New York. Moments before her friend arrived, Tzvi called, and my mother handed the phone to Sarit. Our daughter listened to her father, nodded her head, hung up the phone, and then turned to open the door to her friend to tell her she couldn't go.

Our children are brought to the hospital, and we remain there with our parents and relatives, keeping vigil for hours near Dov. Bikur Cholim arranges for volunteers to come to the waiting room, supplied with board games, books, and snacks to keep our children busy so we can concentrate on Dov. I don't find out who these guardian angels are until much later, so involved am I with the events transpiring in the ICU. After Dov's brush with death early that day, we expect the worst. But the hours pass and, miraculously, he remains stable.

"Why am I here?" Sarit finally asks us. "I should be with my friends in New York. What is the point of me being here?"

"I told you to stay because I thought we were losing Dov," explains Tzvi.

"But he's okay now, right? I mean, he's not dying now."

"No, but we don't know what's going to happen to him. His condition is still very, very serious."

"Why can't I go to New York now?"

Tzvi and I exchange glances. Sarit is, after all, thirteen years old. She wants to be with her friends, and we can't blame her.

"What if something happens?" I finally ask.

"Then you'll call me and I'll take a train home. Or I'll get a ride with someone."

We are silent. The idea of Sarit traveling to New York while our family is in crisis is not appealing. But then again, I think, this is a perfectly reasonable request from a teenager. Why shouldn't she go?

"I have no idea how to get you there," Tzvi finally replies.

Sarit's eyes water. "It's not fair! I've been looking forward to this trip *forever*. And now Dov is in the hospital, and I can't do anything for him by staying here, and still I need to miss my trip! What's the point?"

Tzvi puts his hands on Sarit's shoulders. "I know it's disappointing. Let me talk with Ema and we'll think about it some more."

After she leaves the room, he turns to me. "Why don't we send her to New York? Dov is stable. She could meet up with the group tonight. There's still a day left of touring."

"Dov could die any minute. Then what?"

"Then we'll get her back here somehow."

"Don't you think there might be some psychological repercussions to this? She's only thirteen now, and she doesn't realize what she's asking. What about when she's a little older? Will she ever forgive herself for running off to New York while her brother was dying? Will she ever forgive us for allowing her to do so?"

Tzvi is silent. "Let's ask Eve," he finally replies.

When Eve arrives, we explain the situation. "Do you think it would be detrimental to her if she went on her trip and then her brother died?"

"I don't think so," she says. "You should realize that what you are seeing is a perfectly normal response to trauma from someone her age. Actually, I think, if you can arrange it, it would be good for her to go. Besides, if something happens, she can come back fairly quickly."

But the question of how to get Sarit to New York remains. We are discussing different options when our friend Dr. Edwin Zaghi, who is doing his residency in pediatric dentistry at the hospital, stops in to see how we are doing.

"Is there anything I can help you with?" he asks.

"Yeah," says Tzvi, "do you know anyone who is going to New York today?"

Edwin rubs his chin. "I have a friend who goes fairly often. Maybe he could help. Why?"

I tell him about Sarit's desire to join her friends on their New York trip. Edwin knows all about it; his wife Miriam is one of the teacher chaperones.

"I think my friend might be able to help," Edwin says. "Let me see if it can be arranged."

Within a half hour, Tzvi tells me that someone has agreed to take Sarit by train to New York, where she will be met by Miriam and escorted to her group.

Sarit is elated.

"Who is the person who is taking her?" I whisper to Tzvi.

"Edwin won't say. But I think it's him."

"What?"

Tzvi turns to face me. "I think Edwin has arranged for someone to watch his children so that he can accompany Sarit on a train to New York. Then, after Miriam picks her up, he will take a train straight back."

And that is exactly what happens. Sarit is able to join her friends and enjoy her eighth-grade trip because of Edwin's great kindness in accompanying her on a five-hour train ride to New York so that she won't miss out.

Chapter 16
Wednesday, June 7, 2006

Our eighth day at the hospital is mercifully uneventful. Dov is still in the ICU and his condition is tenuous, but he remains stable. We are surrounded by a special group of family and friends supporting us, but we are nevertheless completely drained.

At some point, Dr. Darren Klugman, who has been tending to Dov throughout his stay, suggests that we take some time to go home. "Go visit your other children," he says. "Take a break."

Tzvi shakes his head. "I'm scared to leave Dov," he replies simply.

Dr. Klugman looks him in the eye. "I will stay with him and take care of him," he says. "I promise. Now go."

So, we do. We head home, hug our children, shower, eat our own food, and rest in our beds. We hear that Sarit has been enjoying her New York trip and will return home in a few hours. For the first time in many days, we feel a tiny sense of peace. We know that the danger has not passed, but for these few hours, we check our worries at the door. Undoubtedly, we expect to carry them again soon, but it's a relief to set them down even temporarily.

Several hours later, we return to find Dr. Klugman at Dov's side. We thank him profusely for his care, and then Tzvi and I set ourselves up to remain in the hospital throughout the night.

That evening, Rabbi Binyamin Krakauer, who works with Tzvi, comes to visit. He stands by Dov's side as we tell him the doctors' bleak prognosis. "Be strong," he says. "Do not lose hope.

"May you dance at Dovie's wedding," he continues. "And may you dance at Dovie's children's weddings."

"Amen," replies Tzvi, as they embrace.

When I was eight, I planned a birthday present for my mother. I hoped that when I was done with it, it would look exactly like the picture on the box that contained the materials and instructions: A circular glass vase hanging from beautifully knotted strands of rope, with cascading vines growing from the vase. We had two plastic vases with fake flowers flowing from them in our den, so I thought that my mother would appreciate a genuine plant. I enjoyed creative projects, and I worked hard on the macramé rope strands.

One day, with my mother's birthday fast approaching, I decided it was time to see how the vase would fit. I removed it from the box and positioned the macramé strands around it. As I lifted the strands to see how it looked, the vase tumbled to my carpeted floor and broke into several pieces.

I gazed at the broken vase in horror. Gone were my hopes of giving my mother anything resembling the perfect project pictured on the box. What could I do? I couldn't just replace the vase; it had to be a specific size to fit the strands and, besides, I had no idea where to look, or how I could afford to buy one. But I certainly couldn't give my mother the woven ropes alone.

I decided that my only hope was to ask God for help. Surely, I thought, God was capable of fixing a broken vase. In the grand scheme of things, I reasoned, this was a tiny request.

I knew how to recite the morning prayers. I prayed hard, asking God to fix it. Every morning, I would add a request to the liturgy: "Please, God," I implored, "fix the vase so I can give my mother her birthday present."

I kept the pieces of the vase wrapped up, stored safely in my desk drawer. I was afraid to check it. I willed myself to believe that if I had faith, God would repair it. For an entire week, I prayed, repeating my request again and again. For an entire week, I resisted the urge to peek and see if the vase had been made whole because of my appeals.

Eventually, with only days left before my mother's birthday, I couldn't wait any longer. I closed the door to my room and locked it. I sat at my desk and slowly opened the desk drawer. Then I took out the box and carefully unwrapped the vase, holding my breath, closing my eyes as the last piece of tissue paper fell away. I believed, with all my heart, that when I opened my eyes, I would see the vase repaired. But when I finally looked, all I found was the same broken vase I had placed in the desk a week earlier. I examined it carefully; maybe at least part of it had been mended? But no, it was exactly what it was before I had started praying: A broken vase, hopelessly beyond repair, and utterly unfit to be my mother's birthday present.

I decided to replace the vase with a plastic cup I found among the bath toys that were kept in the cabinet under our bathroom sink. It was too small, but perhaps it would look prettier once some vines started growing out of it. I planted the seeds included with the kit, but nothing had grown by my mother's birthday. In the end, I gave her the plastic cup, seemingly filled only with dirt, hanging by the beautifully knotted macramé strands I had worked so hard on. And I learned that miracles—even small, seemingly insignificant miracles—don't come easy, even when you pray your hardest. Even when the only one who can possibly solve the problem is God.

I watch Dov, connected to machines that monitor his heartbeat, give him oxygen, and keep him alive. I am decades older now, and he is my broken vase. I will pray with all my heart. I will beg others to do the same. Only God can solve this problem. And yet, in the back of my mind, I hear a tiny eight-year-old voice telling me that all the prayers in the world won't necessarily repair a broken vase.

Chapter 17
Tel Aviv, 1986

"Oh no!" Cindi exclaimed. "My rings are gone!" I exchanged glances with my friends Rachael, Ruchie, and Sharona. It was late on a Saturday night, and we had all grabbed the last bus from Tel Aviv after eating at a fast-food restaurant. We were standing, squashed together and swaying, as the crowded bus made its way back to Petach Tikva, where we were studying. And now Cindi, who had come with us for the outing, had lost something. Not for the first time.

"Are you sure?" I asked her. "Maybe you put them in your bag?"

"No, I know what happened. I took them off to wash my hands. I must have left them on the table in the restaurant, in a napkin. They probably got thrown out!"

I sighed. This was entirely plausible. It was customary to remove rings when ritually washing hands before eating bread, and we had all done that, since we'd ordered hot dogs. It was also quite likely that Cindi had lost the rings; it was not the first time she had lost something. We had been friends since we were twelve and went to high school together, and I had spent a good part of our friendship helping her search for missing wallets, photos, jewelry, money, and clothes. Now we were both eighteen years old, spending our gap year at Orot College in Petach Tikva, Israel, and Cindi's reputation for losing things was becoming legendary even here at our school.

Sharona shrugged and whispered to me, "She's *your* friend."

I gave her a nasty look. It was true that I had known Cindi longer than the others in our group, but that did not make me her guardian, a fact our little clique seemed to forget. "Come on, Cindi," I said. "Did you check your pockets?"

"They're not here," she said, getting more hysterical by the minute. "My mother is going to kill me! She gave me those rings. We have to get off the bus so I can go back to the restaurant."

"Are you crazy?" said Rachael. "This is the last bus! How are we going to get back to Petach Tikva?"

"I need to find my rings!" Cindi cried, getting louder by the second. We had begun to attract attention from the other passengers.

Ruchie hid her face in her hands. Somehow, we always managed to embarrass Ruchie. "Can't you lower your voice?" she hissed.

"Yaffa," Cindi turned to me, "come with me and help me find my rings."

I glanced at the others. The last thing I wanted to do was get off the bus and have to spend the night on the streets of Tel Aviv. "Look, Cindi," I said, "Let's be reasonable. Rachael is right. It's crazy to get off the bus now. Let's get back to Petach Tikva and as soon as we arrive, we'll get to a phone and call the restaurant. I think that's our best bet."

Rachael and Sharona nodded their heads. "Good idea," said Sharona. "I have some extra *asimonim* you can use." In 1986, the only way you could use a public pay phone in Israel was by inserting tokens—*asimonim*—which would be gobbled up quicker and quicker the longer you spoke. We never left our apartment without carrying at least a dozen of them.

But in 1986, it was also possible, we discovered, to start a business without a phone. That was what we found out when we called information after disembarking from our bus at close to 1:00 am. Because the restaurant was a new establishment, the operator told us, it didn't yet have a phone.

We trudged back to our apartment, unsure of what to do next. "I *knew* we should have gotten off the bus," Cindi muttered.

"Getting off the bus would have been crazy," Rachael repeated. "You would have gotten stuck in Tel Aviv for the night."

"But now I don't have my rings! What am I going to tell my mother?"

"Maybe *don't* tell your mother?" I suggested.

"No, I have to get them back. My rings were in the napkin and were probably thrown out with the garbage. I need to get there before the garbage pickup tomorrow, so I can hunt through the trash."

We exchanged glances. "Um, I think the garbage usually gets picked up pretty early," Sharona pointed out.

"Then we'll have to leave at dawn. Yaffa, come with me."

It was not a request, I noticed. "Cindi," I said, "you're insane."

"Yaffa!"

But I had had enough. "You're always losing things, and I'm always trying to fix everything for you! But this...this is *crazy*! Do you honestly expect me to get up at the crack of dawn to travel back to Tel Aviv and help you hunt through garbage? Forget it! I'm done!"

I stormed away from our group. Friendship, I thought, had its limits. Why didn't she ask anyone else? Sharona, Rachael, and Ruchie had all been there too. Why did it always have to be me?

I sat down and closed my eyes. I was exhausted. I truly didn't want to get up before sunrise tomorrow. But then I heard whispering in the background, and some words floated back to where I sat.

"So...*selfish*," I heard. "...supposed to be my friend."

I scowled. There was no getting around this. I walked back to where our group was gathered. "Fine!" I yelled, not caring who heard me. "I'll do it, dammit!"

Sharona nodded her head. "You're a good friend," she whispered.

I gave her a nasty look. *I can't stand it*, I thought.

Before we finally went to sleep, at around two in the morning, Cindi set her alarm. We were planning to be up by four thirty to catch the five o'clock bus and be in downtown Tel Aviv by six. But the next thing I knew, she was shaking me.

"Get up, Yaffa! We overslept!"

I jumped out of bed; it was after five. We dressed hurriedly and rushed out to the bus stop, then boarded the first bus for Tel Aviv that arrived. But even I could tell that it was likely that we were too late; the sun began to rise while we were still on our way. When we reached our stop, we jumped off the bus and ran to the restaurant, only to see the garbage truck driving away in the distance. Nevertheless, Cindi raced towards the garbage dumpsters in back of the building.

Am I really doing this? I thought. *Am I completely out of my mind?*

After only a few moments, she was back, dejected. "They're empty," she said. "We're too late. The garbage has been picked up." She began to cry.

I put my arm around her. "We tried our best."

Cindi wiped her tears. "My mother is going to *kill* me."

"Maybe she won't. Look, she can't do much anyway, right? We're in Israel and she's in New York."

"I need to call her right now and tell her what happened."

"Okay," I said, even though I thought calling her mother right then was a lousy idea. "I'll come with you. It's, what, maybe midnight in New York? And it's Saturday night. Your mother will be up. Good time to call."

We headed for a payphone, and I handed Cindi an *asimon* so she could call the international operator. When Cindi's mother was finally on the line, Cindi started crying again. "I lost my rings, Mommy! I'm so sorry!"

I stood nearby as Cindi listened to her mother.

"What do you mean, 'those old things'?" she said in a completely different tone of voice. "Mommy, I thought you'd be angry with me. You gave those rings to me.... Oh. Okay. Really? Fine. Thank you. I love you, bye!"

I blinked as she hung up. "What was that all about?"

Cindi smoothed her hair. "She said not to worry about it."

"*What?*"

"She said they were cheap rings and she could replace them."

As we stood together, the sun beginning to shine in earnest, I had the distinct urge to strangle Cindi once and for all. But instead, I looked at her, and she looked at me, and together we collapsed in laughter.

"*Cheap rings?*" I could barely get the words out, I was gasping so hard from laughing. "We took the red eye to Tel Aviv to search through the garbage dumpsters for some *cheap rings?*"

"Well, I didn't know they were cheap rings. How upsetting."

It was not the last time I would help Cindi search for lost items. On the way back to the United States, I would run frantically through Ben Gurion Airport looking for the passport she had left at a falafel stand. In college, back in the States, I would help her locate her purse and her wallet several times. Our friends would shake their heads and snicker, teasing Cindi that they wouldn't be surprised if one day, while shopping at a supermarket or visiting an amusement park, Cindi would lose her child. But in one of life's ironic little twists, I, the friend who always dutifully accompanied Cindi in searching for her lost items, would one day sustain the greatest loss of all.

And when that happened, Cindi would be the one to come and hold my hand.

Chapter 18
Thursday morning, June 8, 2006

Cindi Dresdner comes to visit me. She is an immigration lawyer, lives in New Jersey, and is still one of my closest friends. Just two weeks earlier, we had stayed at Cindi's house to attend my brother Akiva's wedding. His wedding was on a Tuesday night in New York, and we hadn't been sure where we could stay. When I contacted Cindi and asked if she would mind hosting us, she had graciously agreed to put us all up.

Now she has taken a train to Washington, D.C., and she stands next to Dov in the ICU as we talk, barely able to comprehend that this is the same boy who so recently played on her Nintendo. As I tell her about everything that has happened, I begin to shiver again.

"You're shaking," she says. "My God."

"I haven't stopped shaking since this happened," I admit.

"Yaffa," she says, holding my hand, "I am so sorry this has happened. There's nothing worse than this. And you and Tzvi don't deserve this."

I show her the thick stack of get-well cards we have received. Included among them is a CD that Sarah has created and sent us from Israel after hearing that Dov could most likely hear our voices.

"Have you listened to that yet?" she asks me.

"No, not yet."

"Maybe now would be a good time. What do you think?"

I turn to Tzvi, who has been sitting with us, and shrug. Why not? We place the CD in the player and listen as the first familiar notes of Survivor's "Eye of the Tiger" play. Sarah is such a riot, I think, and for a few minutes we tap our feet to the music, hoping that perhaps Dov can hear it too. And then we hear the unmistakable voice of Sarah's son Itai, age nine.

"Dovie," he says, "I want you to get better so you can twirl me around the world like you did at Yitzie and Ruthie's house."

And suddenly the memory hits me, hard: It was the Shabbat before Akiva's wedding, and Sarah, her husband Levi, and their children were in from Israel for the occasion. We had decided to meet up at Yitzie and Ruthie's house in New Jersey. Dov was amusing Itai by hoisting him up under the arms and spinning him around the room. And suddenly I am sobbing, as I recall the healthy, carefree, loving young man who horsed around with his cousins, the same young man who lies here today, barely alive.

"Turn it off!" I cry. "Turn it off!"

Cindi removes the CD and cradles me in her arms as I cry. "I guess that wasn't such a good idea after all," she says.

"I guess not," I reply, sniffling.

There is not much to say, even for friends as close as we are. But still Cindi stays, talking not only with me and Tzvi but also with my mother-in-law, before she leaves. "I'll keep on praying for him," she promises.

I embrace her. "Thank you. I cannot thank you enough for coming."

"I had to come."

My father has to fly back to Connecticut, but before he does, he sits with us in Dovie's room. I grew up in a very musical family. My father and mother like to sing, my mother writes songs, my father plays the guitar, and every week of my childhood, without fail, we all sat around the Shabbat table singing and harmonizing as a small choir.

Now my father sits with Dov and begins to sing. The melody lassoes my heart and tugs at it, spinning my head. I cannot comprehend what I am witnessing. Here is my father, who carried me on his shoulders and sang me lullabies before I went to bed, singing a familiar melody to my dying son.

It will be months before I am able to listen to that song again without crying.

We checked Dovie's tefillin already, but my mother keeps on urging me to have Tzvi's tefillin checked too. A friend of hers shared that according to a book she read, a great rabbi once urged someone to do this in order to avoid a tragedy. I suggest the idea to Tzvi.

"I don't want to do it," he replies.

"Why not? We've tried everything else. Why not this?"

"I can't do it."

"Tell me why."

"Yaffa," he begins, "my tefillin are like Dovie's. They are sealed, and never need to be checked."

"Let's check them anyway."

"If I get my tefillin checked, they cannot be opened. They must be broken."

"We can have them fixed."

Tzvi begins to cry. "My tefillin are very special to me. They were a gift from my students." He wipes his eyes. "It wasn't easy for me to have Dovie's tefillin broken, but that's what we were told to do, and so I did it. But this isn't a rabbi who has told us. It's a *book*. It's a *book*! I'm dealing with the very real possibility that I might have to be saying Kaddish for Dov soon. I want to have my tefillin with me. Yaffa, if you tell me to do it, I'll do it. But I don't want to."

"Why? I don't understand."

"Because," he says, "if I lose my tefillin, I'll lose my connection to Hashem. And I cannot bear that. Not now."

I gaze incredulously at my husband, the same man who scoffs at false piety and thinks that long prayer services with never-ending singing are a waste of time.

"You're kidding."

"Do I look like I'm kidding?" Tzvi asks, as tears run down his face. "Do I sound like I'm kidding?"

"I'm sorry. Tzvi, I am so, so sorry." I embrace him and hold him as he cries.

"You tell me what to do," he says. "If it's important to you, I'll get the tefillin checked."

But my decision has already been made. "We're not going to do it. We draw the line here."

Chapter 19
Thursday afternoon, June 8, 2006

It is late afternoon, and my mother suddenly grabs my hands, her face stamped with terror, and pulls me towards the ICU. She does not need to say anything; I know precisely what is happening.

Inside Dov's room, doctors and nurses crowd around him, administering drugs and trying to restart his heart. My mother-in-law stands on the side, watching. I open my siddur and begin to pray. Tzvi is on the phone with a rabbi, relaying information about Dov's status. It seems surreal, but Tzvi has already explained that if any life-and-death decisions need to be made, we would need a reputable rabbi to be on hand to help.

Dr. Santiago sees me and puts a hand on my shoulder. "You can get close to him if you like," he says.

I stop praying. I close my siddur. I reach out and grasp Dov's hand tightly. Around me, there are calls for epinephrine. Dov's blood pressure is almost nonexistent. Again, the doctors try to restart his heart. We continue like this for what seems like hours, all eyes glued to the monitor as we watch Dov's pulse fade, the doctors continuing their attempts to shock life back into him.

Tzvi turns to me while holding onto his phone. "At this point, according to the halacha, we are not required to try to bring him back."

My eyes fill, but I am sure of what needs to be done. "Let him go," I whisper.

Tzvi tells Dr. Santiago to stop resuscitating. I continue to hold Dov's hand, my mother and mother-in-law at my side, as the doctors step back and God steps in to gather Dov's soul. As if in a daze, I hear Dr. Santiago calling the time of death.

"Oh, DOVIE!" wails Tzvi, as he collapses on Dov's body in sobs.

The midrash relates that the great Rabbi Meir lost his two sons on the same day. When his wife, Beruriah, discovered that they had passed away, she covered their bodies and greeted her husband with a halachic question. "If someone lent me a precious jewel, and then he comes to ask for it back, am I required to return it?" she asked.

"Of course!" he answered, stunned that she would even think to ask such an elementary question.

Beruriah carefully led him to their children's bedroom. "These are our precious jewels," she said. "God has given, and God has taken. Blessed be His name!"

Rabbi Meir wept and cried out: "My sons! My teachers!"

As I watch Tzvi collapse in tears, I realize that I know exactly how Rabbi Meir cried. I, however, am numb and hollow. I have been crying for the past nine days, doing everything in my power to help Dov, hoping against hope that the outcome would be different. And now, my son is dead, and I feel as if a piece of my soul has died with him.

Yet we have to make decisions almost immediately. We have asked Tzvi's secretary, Barbara Robbins, to bring the children to the hospital. My parents have informed my siblings, and Yitzie calls me; there are hundreds of people praying for Dov and he wants to tell them that Dov has died. We hold him off.

"Wait until our children are in the car," says Tzvi.

"There are people praying for him right now," Yitzie says. "We have to let them know."

"Yitzie," I say, "our children cannot hear this news from anyone except us. If you announce it on the Internet, someone else might tell them. They *have* to hear it from us."

Tzvi answers his cell phone. "They're in the car," he tells me.

I speak into my cell phone. "Okay, Yitzie, you can send an email now."

In Jewish law, honoring the dead means their body is not left alone for a second before it is buried. Tzvi has asked his friend Shmuel Feld to assist with guarding Dov's body. He arrives.

I stand outside Dov's hospital room as Tzvi makes arrangements. "Do you want to consider burying him in Israel?" he asks me. "Or perhaps in New York, near my father?"

I hesitate. "If we go to Israel, it's going to be several more days before we can go home. We won't be able to bury him until Sunday at the earliest. We have been away from our children for nine days, and I don't think we should be away any more, if we can help it."

"What are you saying?"

"I think we should bury him as quickly as possible and then go home. We need to start the healing process as soon as we possibly can. We should bury him nearby so it can be done tomorrow. That's what I think."

Soon, we will meet with our children in the waiting room, and we will have to explain that, despite all of our efforts and prayers, their oldest brother has died. I will hug Hillel hard as he cries and shakes his head, saying, "He *can't* be dead. He *can't*." And then my mother will hold me, weeping, as they wheel out Dov's body, covered in a sheet. And then I will gather two shopping bags and fill them with the stacks and stacks of get-well cards and posters, the food that our friends brought us, and the clothes that Dov wore. But what I leave behind, in that hospital room, are my hopes.

When we arrive home, we find our house spotless. Our kind neighbors have already covered all the mirrors with sheets in preparation for our mourning. We sit in the dining room, surrounded by our family and neighbors, and discuss plans for the funeral. There are so many details; we can barely comprehend them all. We have already announced that it will take place at 10:00 am the next day, beginning at our shul, and emails have spread the word rapidly. One of us must meet the funeral director early in the morning to choose a plot and a casket. We need to decide who will speak.

In the midst of it all, Barbara Price's son David sits with us and offers suggestions. People will need directions from the shul to the cemetery, he notes. He can print them out for us to distribute. He calls Rabbi Dovid Rosenbaum, the assistant rabbi and Dov's teacher, who comes over to discuss the arrangements with us.

I am not at all sure how a funeral is supposed to run. What is the order of events? What needs to be done and said? And from somewhere deep inside my soul, a little voice wants to know: How ever will I bury my son?

Late that night, my uncle, Walter Reich, who with my aunt Tova had visited us in the hospital and then met us when we returned home, writes an email to my extended family.

Subject: To those who loved Dov

Dear All,

Tova and I just returned from the home Dov had shared with his parents and his siblings, and which is now bereft without him. Earlier, as soon as we got Yitzie's message that Dov's condition had undergone a terrible turn for the worse, we went to the hospital. Alas, by the time we got there, Dov's heart had given out, after so many days of struggle. It was a wonderful heart, made as strong as it could be by your prayers and your hopes. But the trauma he had experienced was massive—beyond any that any heart, or any brain, could endure. The doctors were wonderful, the hospital was wonderful, his parents were wonderful, his siblings were wonderful, and all of you, through your prayers and hopes for him, were wonderful. May his family be comforted among the other mourners of Zion and Jerusalem, and may they and all those who loved Dov never suffer such pain again.

Love,
Walter

Chapter 20
Friday, June 9, 2006

In the morning, we arise early and dress for what will arguably be the darkest day in our lives.

Tzvi goes by himself to choose a plot and casket. In a moment of clarity, he chooses a spot close to the back border of the cemetery, so that my father and brothers, who are Kohanim, can still stand nearby while complying with Jewish laws that prevent them from entering. He signs checks for thousands of dollars to pay for the plot and the funeral expenses; we cannot afford any of it, but we are too numb to care.

I dress the children for their brother's funeral. I do not know what to wear. Some people will be dressed in suits, but as a mourner, I cannot wear leather shoes, and I will have to rip any garment I wear, so I am not inclined to don a fancy outfit. In the end, I select a plain, elastic-waisted black skirt, and a long-sleeved T-shirt which I will not mind parting with. I wear a simple black hat and Keds on my feet. I encourage the children to dress simply as well. As I help tie Noam's sneakers, the house starts to fill with relatives arriving from out of town. Among them is Adina's husband, Avi, who has flown in for the day. I am barely aware of anyone. When Tzvi returns, the children and I pile into the car and drive the half-block to our shul.

If I can just make it past the burial, I think, *I will be okay.* I instinctively block out the images in front of me; I barely notice the people assembled inside and outside the synagogue, or the massive audio speakers standing outside so that people who cannot make it inside the building will be able to hear the speeches. Later, I will be told that nearly two thousand people were present, but in this moment I make a concerted effort to focus only on the few feet in front of me, looking neither to the right or left.

We are led into the coatroom, where we meet with Rabbi Rosenbaum. He guides us as we rip our clothes and bless God, the True Judge. And then, when we hear complete silence outside, Rabbi Rosenbaum nods: It's time for us to go into the synagogue's social hall, where the funeral is scheduled to take place. I take Avichai by the hand and concentrate on forcing one foot in front of the other. Everyone is watching us, but I see no one.

We sit in the front, Tzvi on the right with the boys and men, I on the left with Sarit and Avichai. We face Dov's casket, draped in a tallit. *Does he hear us?* I wonder.

And then we listen to the rabbi, uttering prayers. Tzvi leans over, asking me if I want to speak. Earlier that morning, I had sat at my computer, preparing my words, but I had been unsure whether I would have the emotional strength to speak. But now I know I am able. I nod slightly; he signals to Rabbi Rosenbaum, who calls upon me.

As I stand, I hear a collective gasp rising from the congregation. I bring my papers to the podium, but when I begin to speak, my voice sounds as if it belongs to somebody else, as if it is emanating from some place deep inside of me, which has become embodied in pain.

My dear son Dovie, you have always been a child filled with questions. On your bar mitzvah, which took place in this very room less than two years ago, I talked about your *parsha*, which was Chukat. On that day, I said it's somewhat ironic that a child such as you should be given Parshat Chukat as your bar mitzvah *parsha*. Parshat Chukat begins by talking about the *parah adumah*, the red heifer, which has the power to purify the impure, as well as impurify the pure. It is classified as a *chok*, a statute—something that we are commanded to do even though we cannot explain why. Although truthfully, if you read the beginning of Parshat Chukat, there actually is a specific reason why we are commanded to do it. It says: "This is a statute of the Torah, which God commanded us."

Rashi expounds on these words by saying: *gezeira hi milfanai, ain lecha reshut l'harher achareha*. This is the law, and you have no right to question it.

That's what I told you at your bar mitzvah two years ago. And yet here I stand, in complete shock and utter disbelief, at your funeral! And here we are, Dov, and you, the boy with all the questions, is leaving us with so many, many questions. So many questions that will very likely never be answered.

I have so many questions for the *Ribbono shel Olam*, the Master of the Universe. I want to ask why? Why were you struck down while crossing a street that you had crossed hundreds of times before? Why did it have to happen in front of your school, and in front of our home? Why didn't you just suffer broken bones, a concussion, something that could be repaired? We could have dealt with months or years of rehabilitation. Why did you have to be injured so severely that within an hour of your accident, we were told that there was very likely no hope?

I want to ask: *Ribbono shel olam*, why Dovie? Why take a wonderful, sensitive boy, so committed to Torah and *mitzvot*? Why take a child not yet fifteen years old, with so much more to experience in life?

Dovie, we should have been able to dance at your wedding.

We should have been able to dance at your children's weddings.

Dovie, what are we doing here? You should be studying for finals! We should be getting you ready for camp!

Ribbono shel olam, I just don't get it.

I know, Dov, that one of your truly amazing traits was that you took praying very seriously. You made it your business to always attend *minyan*, and you sometimes grew frustrated when you saw others talking during *tefilla*.

But Dov, I want you to know that you, in your last nine days of life, succeeded in accomplishing what many can never do in a lifetime. After your accident, we heard that hundreds of people from this community came to say Tehillim for you here. We believe that saved your life that night. And then calls, emails, and assistance from all over the world started pouring in. We heard from people who had never opened a siddur before, who began to recite Tehillim for you. We heard from people who are not Jewish, who told us that they, too, were praying for you. We were told of entire schools and communities throughout the world who were praying on your behalf. Dovie, in the last days of your life, you united thousands of people in *tefilla*, *chesed*, and *tzedakah*.

There's a well-known tale about a man who dreamed that he saw footprints in the sand, one set for him, and one set for God, yet he noticed that at the hardest times of his life there was only one set of footsteps—because God was actually carrying him through those times.

I don't think a Jewish person could have written that story. Because Daddy and I have spent the last days seeing footprints in the sand, only in our sand, there are thousands upon thousands of footprints—so many people, so many members of *Am Yisrael*, hoisting us up to carry us through the most difficult nine days of our lives. During the trying days with you in the hospital, when we felt like our hearts were in our mouths, Hashem gave us a very special gift: He gave us the rare opportunity to see the absolute very best in people, and the tremendous strength of *Am Yisrael*.

Dovie, if you only knew how many *mitzvot* were performed in your merit. One of our neighbors kept a notebook filled with pages upon pages of people who volunteered to cook, take care of your siblings, do laundry, and a thousand other things. I wish there was some way to send this book to Hashem, with the plea that nobody else ever undergo the type of pain we are experiencing. How can there possibly be any more harsh decrees for such an extraordinary people?

Dovie, I want to tell you something: I have absolutely no doubts that Hashem heard each and every one of our *tefillot*. He can't possibly not have heard them. Each minute you survived was a miracle to us, a sign that all of those *mitzvot* were having a very real effect on your outcome. We saw with our own eyes the exceptional care you received at the hospital, the tremendous efforts that were taken to save your life. We know, with absolute certainty, that we did every possible thing, both physical and spiritual, to save your life.

We know that today, as we stand here trying to comprehend this tragedy, we can only say, as I said on your bar mitzvah, *gezeira hi milfanai*—this is Hashem's decree. You are our Parshat Chukat. And we don't understand it. We will never understand it. But somehow, we have to accept it.

Dovie, you are loved so much, by your friends, teachers, community and family. We do not know how our family can possibly go on without you.

Dovie, I love you so much.

Later, I will wonder just what prompted me to get up and speak in front of so many people. I detest public speaking. As a distraught mother, nobody would have cared if I had sat silently. But I felt compelled to speak, not just for my community, who sat in dumbfounded shock; not just for my family, who needed to hear these words; and not just for Dovie, who I hoped could still hear me. The truth is that I spoke mostly for my own sake. Because I, more than anyone else in the room, needed to believe those words.

We listen to Rabbi Rosenbaum and Tzvi speak, as well as Rabbi Anemer and my father, who, as Kohanim, are prohibited from entering the room when a dead body is present, and address us by speaking into a microphone hooked up from outside.

Sometime in the middle of it all, Avichai begins to whimper. I hold him on my lap and try to calm him, but it becomes clear that he wants his blanket most of all and, alas, we have left the blanket at home. So, in the middle of one of the speeches, Barbara Price assesses the situation, takes his hand, and leads him home to fetch his beloved blanket. We will pick him up to go to the cemetery later.

When the speeches are over, I look around for the first time and truly see the masses of people who have assembled here today. And then I think of my conversation with Judy the night before, when I confessed to her that I was worried that there would not be enough people to make a *minyan* at the cemetery, and then we would not be able to say Kaddish. At the time, Judy had looked at me as if I had taken leave of my senses. "I think," she said slowly, "that you will not have a problem with a *minyan*."

Later, she will ask me if I had been serious about my concern, and the truth is that yes, I was. I hadn't attended many funerals in my life, but I remembered my father-in-law's, and how we had to make sure that people would come to make up the necessary *minyan*.

But today, clearly, I needn't have worried. We are directed into a waiting car that my brother-in-law Avi is driving. Someone has arranged for a police escort. As we travel down Arcola Avenue onto University Boulevard, and merge onto the Beltway, we can see the stream of vehicles that follow us.

Tzvi is amazed. "A police escort," he says. "Dovie would have been impressed with that."

We have discussed whether or not Avichai should come to the cemetery. I am concerned that he will have nightmares of us burying Dov alive. Tzvi believes that it's important for him to attend. Finally, we agree on a compromise: Avichai comes to the cemetery, but stays in the car with a babysitter and some video games while we attend the burial.

I have heard of people screaming, swearing, crying, and fainting at the burial of their loved ones. A part of me wants to do all of those things. A mother should never have to bury her son. But what I feel most at this point is complete numbness. I have stuffed all of my emotions into some manila file and slammed the cabinet shut, willing myself to deal with it at some other time. Later, that file will burst open in full force, but for now it is safely tucked away, and I shed no tears at this, the most horrific event of my entire life.

I have heard of funerals where the departed is placed in the grave and people walk away, leaving the coffin exposed until funeral workers finish burying the body. This is not the case here. As Dov's body is lowered into the ground, I see the scores of people who have come to pay their respects. These same people grab shovels and help us bury our son.

I watch. Hillel, Noam, and Sarit all take turns shoveling dirt into the grave. I see the director of the summer camp Dov was supposed to attend help bury him as well. My father, who as a Kohen cannot enter the cemetery, stands outside the perimeter and reaches his hands in, clutching a shovel, determined to help us with this excruciating task. My brothers Yitzie and Ari, and my uncles Avi and David do the same. And then Tzvi and I each take shovels, and we bury our son.

And when it is all done, and we have walked between two lines of people who have stood and arranged themselves to wish us comfort, Tzvi, the children, and I pile into the car, where Avichai sits with the babysitter, still playing his video games, and we begin the drive home.

"And now," says Tzvi, turning to me, "we start again."

Part 2

Chapter 21
Shiva

In the mornings, I fight to stay asleep, knowing that as soon as I open my eyes, my nightmare will begin. During my first few seconds of consciousness, I see our large, grand bedroom mirror with its ornate wood frame covered entirely by a white sheet. Reality attacks me like frigid water being poured down my back. *No,* I think, *it can't be true. Can I really be sitting shiva for my son?* Every evening, I silently pray that the next morning I will discover that this was all some elaborate, horrific dream, that Dov will come bounding into my room and complain that he needs better Internet access. That's when I will grab him and hug him tightly, despite his protests, and I will tell him how much I love him, and how he will never get through another day without receiving a hug from me. But the sheet on the mirror dashes all hopes, and I descend into an abyss of despair.

For seven days of shiva, we feel totally humbled, exposed to hundreds of people as mere flesh and blood, trying hard to contend with excruciating, unfathomable pain. We sit in chairs close to the ground, our shirts torn, our hair disheveled and dirty. I wear no makeup. I could use a good, hot shower, and Tzvi could use a shave. I think incredulously of Dov's bar mitzvah, when I shopped months in advance to find the perfect suit, the perfect wig, and the perfect shoes, and how I reupholstered our sofas and dining room chairs in anticipation of the guests who would arrive. Now, hundreds walk through our open door and sit with us. I am told that outside, dozens more are lined up, waiting for their turns to enter. Our air conditioning blows incessantly but cannot cool the house adequately for the swarms of people who have come to extend their condolences. The blinds on the back door need to be replaced, our floor tiles are cracked, and our walls badly need paint, but I don't care. Even if I looked perfect and the house looked perfect, there could not possibly be any semblance of perfection in our home.

Most people sit and say nothing, and I cannot blame them. What can they possibly say? When an elderly person dies, we console ourselves by saying that they lived a long life. When a sick person dies, we tell ourselves that they are finally at peace. But when a young person's life is suddenly, inexplicably, horrifically cut short, there are no words that can possibly console. I look at the silent visitors, and I think that were I in their place, I too would say nothing.

Others do try to engage us in conversation, and I quickly become accustomed to the same well-meaning, meaningless questions being asked over and over again: How are your kids doing? Are you getting any sleep? What can we do to help?

Some want to know details about the accident, but most let us take the lead and discuss what we want, which is a problem, because often we, too, are at a complete loss for words. After a while, I begin to feel as if I am on the verge of insanity; I think that perhaps I will print out a Frequently Asked Questions page and distribute it to everyone so I will not have to repeat myself over and over again.

At one point, I sit before a silent crowd, and feel a mad urge to smack my hands together and proclaim loudly, "So! What shall we talk about today?"

Sarit sits shiva, usually down in the basement, surrounded by her friends and classmates. She has finished eighth grade and should be celebrating her graduation, but she skips her end-of-the-year barbeque and commencement. Hillel, though not yet bar mitzvah, wants to sit shiva as well. He has torn his shirt with too much force, so that the entire front is ripped to the bottom, and it appears as if he is wearing a rag. Noam and Avichai are shuttled around by neighbors who take them to school for their final days before summer vacation and then arrange endless play dates to keep them occupied. My mother-in-law is technically not considered a mourner, but she mourns nevertheless, sitting in a chair at the back of our living room throughout the day.

My neighbors take over my kitchen and man the phones. I feel especially bad for those who call us on the phone; they don't have the luxury of being able to visit us in person and sit quietly in our living room. I make an effort to speak to those who call, to thank them for reaching out, and to tell them how much I appreciate it.

Some people, perhaps because they are at a loss for words, say remarkably stupid things. They mean well, I know, but I don't appreciate it when they tell me that Dov died because he was so good. *Does that mean*, I want to scream, *that I should make sure the rest of my kids are bad*?

Incredibly, others say they are convinced this happened because of *ayin hara*, the evil eye, which some believe can occur because of jealousy. People believe that *ayin hara* has the power to destroy, which is why many, upon sharing good tidings, will add on a "*kinaynahora*" or a "*bli ayin hara*," meaning that there should be no evil eye. I have never bought into the concept; I have always rolled my eyes at what I firmly believe to be an overblown superstition. But now the suggestion triggers a whole slew of theoretical musings in my mind: Maybe it happened during my brother Akiva's wedding, when the entire family was bedecked in beautiful wedding clothes. Perhaps one person looked at us with anger, and wished for something bad to happen to us. Dov had not been the one walking down the aisle, but he was the first grandson on both sides of our families—the perfect target for someone's vicious hate.

What could have prevented it? I ponder the ramifications of having a son who might have been killed because of an *ayin hara.* Maybe I was too nonchalant; did it happen because I didn't say "*kinaynahora*"? And if Dov's death really was the result of an *ayin hara*, does it make sense to continue saying "*bli ayin hara*" when talking about how many children I have, if one is already gone? I try to imagine the conversations:

"How many children do you have?"

"Five."

"*Kinaynahora!*"

"Nope, sorry, too late..."

Then there are some who tell us that losing a child counts as repentance for every sin you ever committed. "Too bad," I whisper to Tzvi. "If we had only known, think what we could have gotten away with!" My mind begins to wander madly with the possibilities. Which sins would I commit? I would wear short shorts and a halter top, I think. While eating a cheeseburger. At McDonalds. On Yom Kippur.

I am going insane, I think. *I am seriously losing my mind.*

We discover that some people believe that it is their responsibility to comfort us, and they stop at nothing in their attempts to accomplish that goal—even though we are nowhere near the point where we can possibly be comforted. On one such occasion, Tzvi realizes that a man who has been sitting in our house for over an hour will not leave unless he is convinced that he's made us feel better.

"Thank you for your words," Tzvi finally tells the man. "You've brought me great comfort."

The man beams and leaves.

It takes a few days until I realize that most people simply want a happy ending. They want to know that there is a Plan; that there is order in the world. And so they try to reassure me that this was meant to be: *He was a pure neshama, a pure soul,* they say. *He had fulfilled his purpose on Earth. This is God's plan.* I hear these postulations, and I have the urge to rip off the sheets covering the mirrors and smash the glass to the ground into a million jagged pieces. I want to shove the photos of Dov's smiling countenance in their stunned faces, and dare them to tell me that this young man was meant to die. *There is no way to understand this!* I want to scream. *There is no good here!*

But there are those who do touch our hearts with their words of comfort. Mothers who have lost children hold my hands, look into my eyes, and tell me it's possible to go on. Dov's friends tell us stories about him that make us laugh. At one point, all of his high school teachers enter the room at once, and my eyes fill with tears, thinking of the time and love they devoted to him in the short time he was with them. When people get up to leave, I often ask them to tell me their names. I have never met so many people in my life.

Every day, we receive stacks of condolence cards and emails. We read them all and treasure them all. We receive a package from a high school in Florida with letters of comfort from the entire ninth grade, who didn't know Dov, but were shaken by the tragedy. We are terribly moved by how many people care. We didn't know we had so many friends.

Even the dead come to extend their condolences. At night, I dream of Dr. David Applebaum, who had been my friend when I volunteered in Shaarei Tzedek Medical Center's emergency room in Jerusalem in 1987. David was a skilled, beloved physician and the type of man who could brighten up a room just by being in it. On the eve of his daughter's wedding, he took her out to a café, and they were both killed by a suicide bomber. The shock of that terrible incident never left me. It was so horrific that it left me wondering if some evil higher powers had conspired together to orchestrate the worst possible scenario imaginable.

His death three years ago had marked the first time in my life that I had felt utterly shaken, faced with a complete and absolute injustice committed against someone close to me. I could not comprehend how something so unspeakably evil could have happened to someone so remarkably good. So it is fitting that now, at the darkest point in my life, David visits me in a dream. We are standing outside the Berman Hebrew Academy auditorium, and I realize that this is where I composed myself two years before, when I created a Yom Hazikaron ceremony in his memory. David says nothing to me now in my dream, but he stands by my side, holds my hand, and silently weeps.

Friends, relatives, and colleagues travel in to see us from all over the country. My siblings Sarah, Elisheva, Shimi, and Yoni fly in from Israel. Our neighbors arrange to have them picked up from nearby airports and brought to us, and then they arrange for them to be housed and fed. One of our friends comes to our house every day and becomes the unofficial shiva bouncer, kindly asking people to leave at noon so we can take a short break to eat lunch. Groups of volunteers arrive before each meal to set up and serve, and we sit at the table while they wait on us and encourage us to eat and drink. Throngs enter our home for the morning and afternoon prayers, and I become accustomed to hearing Tzvi reciting Kaddish, his voice carrying throughout the house.

Judy hands me memos with questions about things she should attend to: Should she arrange to donate the surplus of donuts to the Yeshiva? Which children need play dates? She asks for ways to help, and I tell her what to do: Call Dov's dentist and orthodontist, so we won't need to explain why he won't be keeping his appointments. Cancel his summer camp. Return the clothes I bought for him. I cannot bear to do any of these things. Judy takes notes and assures me it will be done.

And I sit, and talk, and listen, with Tzvi at my side, and a picture of a smiling, innocent Dov hanging behind us.

For Shabbat, our neighbors and friends arrange to house and feed my parents, siblings, and their families so that they can remain with us. Doing this is no simple task: all together, we number more than thirty people. In one extraordinary gesture of kindness out of so many others, I discover that Judy has actually borrowed our cookbooks to gather our favorite recipes and has arranged for people to prepare them. As a result, we are given the comfort of eating familiar food.

On Friday night, our family gathers around several tables, and Tzvi asks my father to make Kiddush. Much later, I will find out why: Tzvi confesses that he simply could not bring himself to praise God.

So involved are we with being comforted that I am rarely able to cry. I talk and talk and talk, and soon it's as if I'm a reporter, relating the same awful story again and again, a story with which everyone is familiar. Only once do I actually shed tears, and this is when Dov's Talmud tutor comes to console us. I have never met him in person before, and it pains me that I am meeting him for the first time now. Once I realize who he is, my eyes suddenly fill with tears, and I drop my head into my hands and begin to sob. "So much learning!" I cry, thinking of the hours Dov spent trying to figure out a page of Talmud. "So much learning, and for what? For what? Tell me," and I wipe my eyes and turn to Dov's tutor. "Tell me. What was it like to learn with him?"

And his tutor tells us about the constant question-and-answer sessions they would have, Dov's incessant challenging, the thirst for learning that characterized so much of who he was. I wipe my eyes and look around the room at the crowd that sits silently, listening to our exchange and not knowing what to say. The scene is surreal. What can they possibly say?

And that night, I return to my room exhausted, as I have done every night of shiva, and stare at my mirror covered in a white sheet. *Let this be a dream*, I think. *Let me go to sleep tonight and wake up to my normal life. Let me go to sleep and wake up knowing that all of my children are alive and well. This week cannot possibly be real.*

And yet it is.

Chapter 22
The Driver

Several days into our shiva, Barbara Robbins beckons for me to stand up and follow her, and I obey. When we have put some distance between us and the crowd of visitors in the living room, she leans over and whispers in my ear, "The driver is here."

She does not need to elaborate; I know exactly which driver she is referring to. I draw a deep breath. "Where is she?"

"Waiting outside. She came with some family. She asked for permission to come and see you."

I signal to Tzvi to join us and tell him who is outside. "What do you think?"

"Yaffa, this is not a good idea."

But I have been thinking long and hard about the driver. I wake up each morning and think that, as badly as I feel, I imagine the driver feels worse. A person can come to terms with grief, but guilt can kill you. In my mind, I run through the possible scenarios.

The driver enters, flanked by several others, whom I presume to be her family. What little conversation was taking place in our living room comes to an abrupt halt. No introductions are needed; everyone, it seems, has deduced just who this woman is, and why she is here.

She approaches me. "I came to tell you that I'm so very sorry for your loss," she says.

My heart is beating wildly as I give her a slight nod. I glance at Tzvi and see that his eyes are wet.

"I also came to tell you that there was nothing I could have done to prevent that accident. I would have stopped if I could. Your son just came out of nowhere."

I glance at Tzvi and see that his eyes, that had been misted with tears, are now glaring. "Our son was a careful boy," he replies. "He lived here most of his life. He knew how to cross the street."

The woman is clearly caught off guard by Tzvi's response. "All I'm saying," she stammers, "is that I wish it hadn't happened."

"But not that it was your fault, right?" snaps Tzvi.

"You terrible woman!" cries a voice from the back of the room, which I recognize as belonging to my mother-in-law. "You killed my grandson! How dare you come in here and say that you couldn't have prevented it?"

I jump to my feet. "Mom!"

"How fast were you driving?" Tzvi demands. "Were you talking on your cell phone? Don't you realize that there's a school here and that people cross here all the time?"

Now I face him, shocked. "Tzvi!"

"How dare you come here with your Christian idea of forgiveness, trying to absolve yourself of the death of our child! Do you think you can simply say you're sorry and let Jesus take away your guilt? You need to do more than say you're sorry. You need to make amends! In Judaism, you would be exiled—you would leave the comfort of your home and fear that someone would avenge my son's death. When you are ready for that, you may beg forgiveness!"

"I said ENOUGH!" I scream. "She came here to extend condolences."

"That's right, Ma'am, that's why I'm here," she says, and I see she is crying.

"Please!" Tzvi replies. "She came here to make herself feel better."

I turn to Barbara, who stands off to the side, looking as stunned as I am. "Barbara, please..." I whisper.

"My grandson was an angel!" cries my mother-in-law. "You killed him! How dare you!"

Barbara meets my eyes, and as always, knows precisely what to say. "Perhaps it's best if you come back after the family has had some time," she tells the woman, as sweetly as possible.

"Yes, please leave!" Tzvi snaps.

The driver stands, her face streaked with tears, her arms held on either side by her relatives. Quickly, Barbara escorts her out, followed by her family, and for several minutes all I can hear are her muffled sobs and my pounding heart.

And then, my mind plays out scenario two.

The driver approaches us where we sit in our low mourning chairs, and then, to my surprise, she drops to her knees.

"I just want to say," she begins, and then suddenly, she starts to weep.

My eyes fill with tears, and I look around the room and see that everyone watching is visibly moved by this sincere display of remorse. I wipe my eyes and lean over to touch her shoulder. "Please," I say, "there's no need to kneel. Please, sit down."

She shakes her head, her hands on her temple. "No," she replies. "Not until I've asked you for forgiveness for the awful thing I have done to your son and to your family. I've relived that accident a million times since it happened. I keep thinking about what I might have done differently."

She bows her head and sobs, and both Tzvi and I cry with her. After a few minutes, she takes a deep breath, and when she speaks, her words are laced with anguish. "I just want to say that I am sorry. Oh, God, I am so sorry! I would not blame you for not forgiving me. I am sure I will never forgive myself."

"Please," says Tzvi, "get off your knees. You are welcome to sit down in our home."

"No, I could not," she replies. "I've done what I came to do." She gives a slight nod to her family members, who help lift her to her feet. Tzvi and I exchange glances and rise from our seats, so close to the floor.

"Thank you for coming," I tell her. "Your words mean a lot to us."

"It could not have been easy for you to face us," agrees Tzvi. "We appreciate that you came."

She gives a slight nod, wipes her tears, and shuffles out the door. In the back of the room, I see that even my mother-in-law is crying.

I glance around the room, and suddenly, a great fear overtakes me. Will she ask for our forgiveness? Or will she say that it wasn't her fault, and that Dov was entirely to blame? I have been trying to keep my composure throughout this dreadful week. Our living room is crowded with visitors. Am I prepared for a possible public confrontation? "I don't know if I can handle this right now."

"You're in charge here," says Barbara. "You do what feels right to you. I can tell her that it's too soon, that she should give you a bit more time and contact you at a later date."

"I think that's a good idea," says Tzvi. "Yaffa?"

I feel dazed. Slowly, I nod my consent.

After the shiva ended, I waited to hear from her, but she never attempted to contact us again. For many months afterwards, I played out the drama and emotion of meeting and confronting her in the safety of my mind, always wondering: What sort of opportunity did we miss by refusing her request to enter? Or what sort of horrific scene did we avoid?

The next time I had the opportunity to see her was in court.

Chapter 23
The *Bris*

O n the fifth day of shiva, my mother tells us that my sister Adina has given birth to a son. The joyous news is a ray of light during our dark week of mourning, but Adina is inconsolable. Even though she has been in constant communication with me by phone throughout this ordeal, and her husband Avi flew from Miami to attend the funeral, she feels awful that she could not physically be with us during this time. And now she fears that her son's birth will only exacerbate our grief.

We speak on the phone, and she asks me about naming the baby after Dov. I have mixed feelings. The custom of naming a child after the deceased is said to be a great comfort, but right now, the pain is so raw that the thought of a new baby carrying Dov's name makes me shudder. I speak to Tzvi and we agree: it's too soon to use Dov's name, and this is what I tell Adina. But, regardless of what this baby will be named, I decide that I want to be at his *bris*.

Not that it will be easy. The *bris* will take place soon after we get up from shiva. I feel utterly broken, and am not sure how well I will manage attending a happy occasion. My emotions are erratic and unpredictable. Will I break down sobbing during the ceremony? Will my presence make everyone uncomfortable? I am a walking tragedy, after all; a reminder of just how easy it is to lose a child. What business do I have attending a ceremony to mark the beginning of a baby's Jewish life? Despite all these considerations, I am determined to go. My sister is my best friend, and I have missed her presence. She was not able to come to me, but I can go to her.

On the last morning of our shiva, just a handful of visitors remain in our living room. As much as our family appreciated all the support and the love, we are all ready to finally close our front door. I have booked my flight to Florida, and Tzvi will be taking care of the children for the three days I will be there.

On the day I leave, Judy is kind enough to drop me off at the airport early in the morning.

"Will you be okay?" she asks.

"I don't know. I hope so."

But I spend most of the flight weeping. I look at the other passengers and feel as if I'm peering into an alternate reality, a place where people are happy and living their lives without pain. I cannot imagine ever being part of that world again. Grief surrounds and envelops me, and yet still, I want to go to my new nephew's *bris*.

When Adina and I finally meet, we embrace and cry together. The baby is beautiful, and I tell her so. Later, we go to the *bris*, and I am struck by how one life can be inexplicably snuffed out at the same time that another is just beginning. I have attended many a *bris* before, but I feel like I am seeing this one with new eyes.

The name of the baby is announced: Binyamin Simcha, a name commemorating the loss of Dov in a unique way. Adina and Avi explain that they chose the name Binyamin because, in the Bible, Benjamin was born as Rachel died, and she originally called him Ben-oni, or "Son of my Sorrow." But Jacob changed his name to Binyamin, or "Son of my Strength." Jacob recognized that with sorrow, comes strength. As for the name Simcha, which means "happiness," they chose it because they truly felt that our family needed to receive some joy.

It is a beautiful and fitting name. I wipe tears from my eyes, and will myself to not break down completely.

Not long after I return home, I receive an email from Adina:

> It was really wonderful to see you at the *bris*. I don't know if I thanked you enough for that. I know how difficult it must have been for you. Actually, come to think of it, I haven't a clue how difficult it must have been. Each time I try and put myself in your shoes I find that I am overwhelmed by the circumstances and can't even begin to fathom what has happened. How much more so for you, Yaffa. And for everyone else. But I know that flying down here to be with us during our *simcha* had to be tough. And I also know that you did it primarily for me. I truly am grateful. It was a relief to see you. To see you intact, despite my worst fears. To see you with a fleeting smile on your face—something I didn't think I would see for a while. Not that it could mean much to you now, but having you there confirmed for me that it was okay to be happy, to find happiness even during such tragedy.
>
> I'm not intending to comfort you here, mind you. I can't even attempt that, knowing that there is little to say that will bring you any comfort or fill the hole that is left in your life. But I wanted you to know that you actually comforted me. A bit of a reversal of roles here, but had to mention it. I don't know if that was your intention coming down here, but it was the result. For weeks, all I wanted to do was fly to Silver Spring and do something to help you. Watch your kids. Clean your house. Hold your hand. I remembered how you stayed with me when Gavriel was born. Most of the advice you gave me about kids I use all the time and quote repeatedly ("Take a shower." "Don't wake the baby." "Get a swing and a pacifier before anything else."—hey, don't laugh. Those are very important words of wisdom!) I wanted to impart some wisdom,

some advice to you, even though deep down I knew that there were no words. No way to halt the pain. No magic phrase, no movie-quote that could stave off the hurt. Even if I prayed for Hashem to give the pain to me, it would not have happened. Much as I wanted it to be taken from you.

Not that it means much, but I do have confidence in you. I know that you will get through this. I even think you know that you will. One day. In time. Not get over it, actually, but perhaps get used to it. Not really move on with life, rather, start over in a new life. On this new path that Hashem has thrown you to. I don't know why, but all I can do is assume that there is a reason—a grander plan—that someday, maybe, we'll all understand.

Attending Binyamin Simcha's *bris* is one of the most difficult steps I ever take. But in the months and years that follow, I always look back on my trip to Miami as proof that it is possible to embrace joy even when our hearts are breaking. This, I discover, is the way we go on living.

Chapter 24
Dov's Birth - June 19, 1991

When my waters break during the night, my obstetrician tells me to head for the hospital once I am no longer smiling. Sixteen hours later, as contractions sear through my body around 6:00 pm, I go to the hospital and am promptly given an epidural. By 4:00 am, I am at ten centimeters, but the baby isn't descending.

I push and push until I am sure that my internal organs will be delivered before this baby. After three hours, the doctor concludes that the baby is in a posterior position and isn't descending; I will need a cesarean. I refuse to accept this. My mother delivered nine children vaginally, and I most certainly can do the same. I tell him I want to push more, and so I do, until the doctors change shifts at 9:00 am. By then, I have been pushing for five hours, and the baby is no closer to being delivered.

"I think you need to understand the risks of doing this," says the new doctor on call.

"*Risks*? What are you talking about?" I cry. "The last doctor said it was okay to keep pushing."

"There's a limit to how much you can keep this up. You're putting your baby at risk."

I cannot continue; I am exhausted from labor, I have received three epidurals, and I cannot argue with the doctor. "Fine," I say. "Just do it."

"Yaffa, are you sure?" asks Tzvi, who has been at my side the entire time.

"I can't take this anymore. Just let them do it."

The doctors prepare for surgery and administer another epidural. After a few minutes, the anesthesiologist asks if I can feel his hand.

"Yes," I say.

Silence. The doctor is dubious. "Let's try this again," he says. "Can you feel this?"

"Yes, I can.... Ouch!"

The doctor shakes his head. "The epidural is not taking. We will need to give you a general."

I am too tired to argue, too tired to insist that Tzvi remains in the room, too tired to care when they put the mask over my face and tell me to breathe deeply. The next thing I know, I am waking up to Tzvi's voice. "Yaffa, it's a boy! A boy! Look!"

I am bleary-eyed, but I get a glimpse of Dov: He looks beautiful. He looks perfect.

"A boy," I repeat in a whisper, because that is all that emerges from my throat. "Tzvi..." I call, as I feel a terrible sensation traveling throughout my body.

"Yes?"

I beckon to him to lean closer; it is the only way he will hear what I am about to say. "*Pain*," I whisper.

Having general anesthesia has its disadvantages, I discover. In my case, it means that, having woken up from surgery, I feel as if I have been cut in half. I am still on the operating table when this horrific sensation overtakes me. This, I think, is what it feels like to be stabbed. I cannot move; even a millimeter of movement, and I feel like my abdomen is on fire. I try hard to remain absolutely still, but it is no use; as they wheel me to my hospital room, I stifle a wail at every small bump the gurney hits on the floor. Finally, when we arrive, a nurse instructs me to move onto my bed.

"I can't do it," I say.

"Yes you can," she replies. "Just move your legs and hop on."

"I can't. I *can't!*"

The nurse calls for help, and she and an aide lift me off the gurney. The searing pain is the most excruciating I have ever experienced. A thousand jolts of lightning tear through me at once. I wonder if the doctors have sliced through me completely. I weep in agony as they place me on the bed, and that is when I think about labor and delivery, and I wonder: *Why would any woman go through this more than once?*

It will be many hours before I speak, or hold my newborn son, and many months before I recuperate from the trauma, both physical and emotional, of the surgery. On the day of Dov's *bris*, I have to go back to the doctor because my incision has become infected, and it will be weeks before I am able to lie down and nurse comfortably.

Dov enters the world amidst great pain. Later, it will occur to me that he exits it in much the same way.

Chapter 25
Grief

Once I return from Miami, it feels like life should be starting again. I am relieved that shiva is over. In the back of my head, perhaps naively, I hope we can get into a normal routine, where we are eating our own meals and driving our own carpools. We certainly don't have to; Judy assures me that she has lists of people who, she says, are just *aching* to prepare meals for us for as long as we want. Meanwhile, our freezer is already overflowing with meals that should last us for the next few months. Just say the word, Judy tells me, and we can forget about cooking for as long as we like.

Really, what is it with Jews and food?

But I am determined to cut the cord, at least in this area. "We need to restore some normalcy to our lives," I explain. "And one of the most basic ways of doing that is for us to prepare and eat our own food, rather than depending on others."

"Well, let me know if you change your mind," she says.

But I don't. I think of the nurses who urged me to get up and walk the day after Dov was born, even though the incision from the cesarean throbbed with unbearable pain. "The sooner you start walking," they explained, "the sooner you will heal." Now, something tells me that, difficult as it may be, I must do the same here: I must learn to walk through life while carrying this pain.

But I quickly discover that this is no easy task, because the pain is everywhere. The food I used to happily cook for my family is now tainted with memories of Dov's appetite. He used to beg me to make potato kugel, and when I did, he would ask for three or four helpings at a time. Now I prepare potato kugel and realize that nobody eats it quite like Dov did; there is a lot left over. I place the half-full pan in the refrigerator and it sits there for days, covered in its shiny tin foil—a painful reminder of our loss. Every time I open the refrigerator I see it, and my heart breaks anew. If Dov were still alive, there would be no kugel left to put in the fridge.

The grief attacks suddenly, without warning, at times when I least expect it. I peel carrots for chicken soup—another favorite dish of Dov's—and all at once I am leaning on the refrigerator, my head bowed, as my shoulders shake with sobs.

The pain extends beyond food. I find I can no longer bring myself to sit in the front of the house, where I can see the traffic passing on Arcola Avenue. Instead, I sit in the kitchen, or the study, which faces our backyard, or in extreme cases, I sit in the front-facing dining room with the blinds tightly shut. I cannot enter Dov's room; the mere sight of his freshly laundered clothes folded in his dresser makes my throat constrict, and I close my eyes, trying to suppress the tears, before I close the door.

Here is what I learn about deep, visceral, gut-wrenching grief: It has the power to rob you of every pleasure you ever thought you enjoyed. My appetite disappears, and foods I previously savored now taste bland. Hunger is my only reminder that I am supposed to eat, and then I gingerly swallow a few morsels, just enough to quiet the rumblings of my stomach. I have always struggled to lose weight, and now the pounds disappear without me realizing it until I can scarcely believe the numbers that appear on the scale. I joke that I have discovered the most effective weight-loss plan of all: the Trauma Diet. It works very well, I tell people, but I wouldn't recommend it.

I have no patience for television. The sitcoms that once made me laugh now seem exceptionally inane and utterly removed from reality. The only program I can bear to watch is the news, and then I watch the reports of crime, murder, and accidents, and I recognize, sadly, that *that* is the real world, filled with horror I never really fully comprehended or acknowledged until Dov died.

I used to love movies, and one evening Tzvi and I decide to go see *Superman Returns*. We ask Sarit to babysit and we set off for our evening together only to find ourselves sitting in the movie theater watching the credits roll, and both of us are in tears. This is a movie Dov would have loved to see, we know, and he is not here to see it. When we arrive home, we park in our driveway, and upon seeing our basketball hoop, I begin to cry again. Dov helped build that basketball hoop, and now he is not here to use it.

I used to love to read. I would look forward to visiting the public library, where I would stock up on novels that I'd devour while curled up on the sofa. Now I start reading books but cannot finish them; I have simply lost the desire to ponder what might happen in a fictional world. In the mornings, I read the newspaper, but I stop reading the comics. Well-meaning friends give me books about grief and suffering, and these I read carefully, although none really answer the question that haunts me most: Why did this happen to us?

The pain lives with us in our bedroom, where Tzvi and I spend our nights holding each other in bed, convulsing with sobs.

And music? Music is the worst of all. If I hear a song that Dov liked, I cannot control the tears. Hearing the theme song of a movie he once enjoyed sends me running out of the room in search of a quiet place to weep. I used to work in my kitchen while listening to music, but now I cannot; the music pierces my heart like daggers. I feel every stab, until finally I change the dial on the radio to a news station, and there it stays.

One Saturday evening, I make the mistake of listening to Idan Raichel while driving in the car, and I break down so completely that I am forced to pull over. I sit in my parked car, heaving with sobs, until there is a knock on my window. Stunned, I see the face of an acquaintance, who explains that she recognized my vehicle and thought I might be having car trouble. I catch my breath before I respond, "I just need a few minutes." She takes one look at my tear-stained face and comprehends, leaving me alone with my heartache. She calls me the next day, asking if there is anything she can do to help. I thank her—and mean it—but can't offer any suggestions.

The pain materializes everywhere: I return to my job as an editor at a children's magazine, but several times a day I have to shut the door to my office so I can cry in private. I tidy up our playroom and I wipe away tears, realizing that the hundreds of Lego bricks we bought for Dov during his short life have actually outlived him. I am paying a bill or thinking about doing laundry and suddenly, the grief appears, like a sudden wave rising from a calm sea, leaving me shivering and cold, my horror mounting as I realize, once again, that the worst has happened, and that it cannot be changed. On these occasions, I have the urge to break dishes and glasses and scream and scream and scream. *My child is dead*! I want to wail in anguish. *I have lost my son*! These bouts of despair can destroy me. I attempt to go to shul on Shabbat, and the familiar prayers, combined with Dov's absence—I would often peek at him, standing tall beyond the *mechitza*—send me home in the middle of the service. I run upstairs to my bedroom and sit on the floor by my bed, weeping like a baby. Another time I see the teenage son of a friend of mine giving his mother a heartfelt hug, and I excuse myself abruptly. I simply cannot bear witnessing such affection when I know I will never be able to embrace Dov again.

A part of me is still in denial. When the phone rings, I imagine it will be Dov, telling us that the whole accident was some sort of elaborate charade, and that he is alive and well. When I see boys riding bikes, I scrutinize them carefully because a small part of me still hopes that one of them will be Dov.

I witnessed the death of my son, I saw him lifeless and pale, I touched his cold skin, and yet still I cannot accept that he is truly and completely gone.

One day, I look in the mirror and notice that my eyes have grown noticeably lighter. They used to be a deep, dark brown, but they have lightened to a hazel-like color. I tell Tzvi of the phenomenon and suggest that since eyes are said to reflect the soul, perhaps my eyes have lightened because Dov's death has in some way altered my soul.

Tzvi has a theory of his own. "Maybe," he says, "you cried out some of the pigment."

One morning, after the children have left for school, I am sitting in the quiet kitchen, stirring my coffee and wiping away the tears which I am accustomed to shedding before heading to work, when I realize I am not alone: Two birds sit directly outside my kitchen window, so close that if I reached out, I would be able to touch them. In fact, I could swear they are watching me. They remain by the window, and we eye each other for several minutes before they fly off.

The incident is so bizarre that later I search for an image of the birds on the Internet just to find out what they are called. My research yields a startling answer: They are mourning doves. How apt, I think. The mourning doves have come to watch me mourning Dov.

Chapter 26
The Binder

I decide to embark on a new project: I gather the stacks of condolence cards and print out reams of heartfelt emails, and begin inserting them into plastic page protectors in a four-inch binder. The work, I find, is painful and painstaking. There are hundreds of messages, some that I only glanced at before, and some that I have not read at all. Now I take the time to sit and read each one carefully before including it in the binder.

"Dov was a friend of mine..."

"I am so sorry for your catastrophic loss..."

"There are no words for such a tragedy..."

There are messages from high school buddies who have been out of touch with us for years. There are cards from strangers who have lost children and are reaching out to us because they have been where we are. From relatives I have met only two or three times in my life.

Yitzie has also printed out pages of emails sent and received, both when Dov was in the hospital and immediately after his death. The pile is several inches thick and includes messages from people—many of whom are strangers—from across the world.

I decide to sort them by date. Slowly, I begin to form a record of the tragic event that shattered our lives so suddenly. I see the email sent from the Yeshiva almost immediately after the accident, telling people to pray for Dov. I read the messages posted by shuls and schools urging people to attend the community-wide

Tehillim on the first night he was in the hospital. I see Yitzie's updates to families and friends, his request for 24-hour prayers, the responses of hundreds promising to help. I read emails from the Berman Hebrew Academy and the Yeshiva offering guidance on how to discuss the accident with children. As I sift through the mountain of paper, I begin to grasp how Dov's death has shaken our family, our friends, indeed, our very community, to its core.

Within days, it becomes clear that one binder will not be enough. I buy three more. I fill one with messages from when Dov was in the hospital, one with condolence emails, and two with cards. I leave empty pages at the end, expecting that there will be more to add.

At night, I dream Dov is sitting at our dining room table, reading the binders. He turns the plastic-coated pages with a look of wonder on his face. Shaking his head in disbelief, he addresses me. "This is *ridiculous*," he says.

And indeed, it is. Who would have thought that so many people cared about Dov, the shy, quiet, cautious boy who once thought he had no friends? Who would have guessed that he would die at such a young age? Who could have predicted, even a month ago, that I would become a bereaved parent? During the occasional moments when I am not wracked with pain, this is the sensible and obvious thought that keeps on making its way into my consciousness: This situation is absolutely unbelievable. It is *crazy*. There is no way we could have expected anything like this to ever occur.

When I have finished working on the binders, I insert photos of Dov in the covers. Then I place all four binders atop our coffee table, where I expect they will remain forever. It is my shrine to Dov and my reassurance to myself; a tangible reminder of how greatly he will be missed, and how desperately we fought for him to live.

But of course, I am a mother, and so another part of me believes that, no matter how unlikely the situation, I should have known. Somehow, I *should* have been able to prevent it.

Over time, I become convinced that Dov's accident couldn't have just occurred; there must have been some warning that I didn't heed. And as I search my memories for clues, more and more flood back to me. I remember an incident that occurred before the accident: On Shabbat, Dov was horsing around with his friend, Ari Rosenberg. Ari chased him outside, and when Dov came back inside, he entered the house quickly and slammed the front door. I heard a crash, and when I opened the door to see what had happened, there stood Ari, looking at the ground, at the plaque that had been hanging on our door. Years before, I had created the plaque with great care and love at a camp woodworking activity: It was a stained-wood oval with a picture of a house, and the words "Klugerman Family— Welcome" written in Hebrew.

The plaque was split, perfectly, down the middle.

I had scolded Dov for ruining the plaque and later, I told him that I wanted him to fix it for me in time for Mother's Day, or buy me a new one. He agreed and took it up to his room. After he died, I found the plaque in his room, still split down the middle. *It was a sign,* I think, *that our family as we knew it was about to be destroyed.*

Next, I remember a bizarre incident that had taken place at work. After Tzvi and I concluded that we needed to request financial aid to help pay Dov's Yeshiva tuition, I had pored over the forms and then spent hours filling them out. I was about to mail the envelope at work, when I felt the urge to correct a few figures on the form. I reached for my white-out, squeezed the small bottle—and it exploded.

My skirt and blouse were covered with tiny white dots. The white-out coated my chair and desk. I couldn't remove all of it; some was still there even now. When it happened, I had decided that some otherworldly presence was trying to send a message to me, and that message was: *send in the damn financial aid form already.* I sealed the envelope and put it in the mailbox, still pondering the unlikely probability of an exploding white-out bottle.

Clearly, God was trying to tell me something. Now I think I should have been able to figure it out. Someone, in some other dimension, perhaps my grandmother or some other departed soul, was trying to send me a warning. I was filling out a form for Dov. And Dov was about to be erased. *Why didn't I see it?* I ask myself in agony. *How could I not have known?*

Then I remembered that for weeks, I had suffered the most intense headaches I had ever had. The pain was so great that it would wake me up in the middle of the night and I would leap out of my bed, clutching my temples, to reach blindly for a painkiller. Several days before the accident, I had visited my doctor, who measured my blood pressure and told me it was way too high. This was a first for me. He recommended an MRI. I stopped wearing my contact lenses, thinking that glasses would help me manage the headaches better.

After the accident, the headaches inexplicably ceased. My blood pressure returned to normal. And the MRI, when I had it, was perfect.

I also experienced what I can only describe as touches of prophecy. During the months leading up to the accident, usually when I was driving, I would have flashes of imagination in which I would inexplicably see myself sitting shiva in my living room, with dozens of students coming to visit me. I would shrug off these awful scenes by telling myself that I was simply worried about Tzvi working long hours, and that this was how my worry was manifesting itself: envisioning sitting shiva for him. It never even occurred to me that these scenes were me sitting shiva for my son.

And then, one Friday night, a few weeks before the accident, as I sat on my bed, completely awake, I "saw" a scene so clear that I began to weep: I was mourning for Dov. I was screaming at the top of my lungs. He was dead, and I could not stop crying. That was the vision, and as I witnessed it I began crying in reality too, tears cascading down my cheeks, even though I knew Dov was alive and well and sleeping in his bedroom down the hall.

The scene my imagination had presented to me was so real that when the doctors told us that Dov would not survive, a small part of me was not surprised.

I think of these incidents, and I must admit that there were indeed signs. Why didn't I heed them? The answer is quite simple: Even if God Himself had warned me of what was about to occur, I would never have believed it. I simply would not have ever believed it.

Chapter 27
Finding Meaning

Since Dovie died, many *tzedakah* donations have been given in his memory. One major recipient has been the Melvin J. Berman Hebrew Academy, where Tzvi works as middle school principal, and which Dovie attended for most of his life. Not long after Dovie's death, the development director approaches us to ask whether there was something in particular we would like the money to be used for.

Tzvi comes up with an extraordinary plan. More than anything, he explains, he would like to use the funds to dedicate a Sefer Torah to the middle school in memory of Dovie. The gesture is extremely meaningful. Having a Torah dedicated in someone's memory is a tremendous honor, and is perhaps one of the most poignant ways to truly focus on life.

A new Torah can cost tens of thousands of dollars, however, and purchasing one would require more money than has been donated, but Tzvi is undeterred. He finds a scribe, a *sofer*, who doesn't just write new *sifrei* Torah, but restores old ones. I accompany Tzvi to the bookstore, where the *sofer* has brought two Torah scrolls for us to see. Both are in need of repair, but in relatively good condition. Tzvi carefully inspects the calligraphy; it must be clear enough for middle school students to be able to read it. He also picks each one up; the lighter one is preferable, so the students will be able to carry it.

"That's the one," he says, pointing at the smaller Torah. I agree.

Restoring an old Sefer Torah is a much more affordable option than commissioning an entirely new one to be written, but it's still a major project. The *sofer* will need to inspect over 300,000 letters, and make sure that the parchment is viable. Since the Sefer Torah is old, some of the letters might be cracked or faded; those letters will need to be rewritten. What's more, we will still need to raise funds beyond the donations already given in Dovie's honor to pay for it. With the school's blessing and help, we embark on an ambitious campaign to turn Tzvi's idea into a reality. We write to the entire Greater Washington Jewish community—the schools and the shuls—and also reach out to our families, offering the option to sponsor individual letters in the Torah at a relatively low cost. They are invited to dedicate the letters in honor of anyone they choose. Hundreds respond with donations.

The funds are used primarily to pay for the restoration of the Torah, but so much is raised that we also plan to purchase a new *mantle*, *gartel*, and *magen*. Tzvi and I select a *mantle* embroidered with a picture of a tree, and the words "*Etz chaim hee lamachazikim ba*—It is a tree of life to those who cleave to it." It is exactly the type of message we wish to convey: our son might be gone, but despite this, we are doing our best to focus on life.

Meanwhile, I decide to take on an ambitious project of my own. Inspired by our experience in the hospital with Dov, when hundreds of people offered to pray for him at all hours of the day, I am encouraged by my siblings to create a website to help families experiencing crisis or illness. The website will function as a network of support and prayer, providing online resources for patients and those who wish to help, the ability to sign up for prayer at specific hours, and a search feature allowing anyone to find someone to support using parameters such as age, illness, or community.

I call the website Dov's List, and almost immediately, people hear of it and start sending us contributions. In particular, the Avi Chai Foundation, which funds the children's magazine that I work for, provides a very generous donation to build the website. Adina puts me in touch with Charly Ohana, a good friend of hers in Florida who is a talented web designer. I talk with Charly by phone, and he is honored to be a part of the efforts. We begin emailing on a regular basis and exchanging ideas.

I have never written website text before, but now I begin working on the home page. Even though creating Dov's List will be a long, demanding project that will take many months, there's something very empowering about channeling grief to create something good. I realize that I now know what people in crisis need, and I can use that knowledge to help others.

Nevertheless, writing the material for Dov's List is emotionally draining. I still can't quite believe that I am working on a project in memory of our dead son.

Chapter 28
The Paper Bag

Detective Murphy has informed me that he will be dropping off some items that were needed for the investigation of the accident. Late in the afternoon, he arrives with a plain paper bag that contains one of Dov's sneakers and his yarmulke. Both were knocked off Dov's body with such force that they were found dozens of feet away from him.

As the detective hands me the paper bag, I wonder what I will do with the items. They belonged to Dov, and he was wearing them when he was struck, so they seem sacred. But they are unlike Dov's Lego sets and computer, which he enjoyed. Instead, they are inexorably tied to the tragedy of his death. I cannot even bring myself to open the bag. What does one do with such items? Bury them? Burn them? Place them in a keepsake box?

"What is going to happen to the driver?" I ask.

The detective glances at his notes. "She was found to be speeding. She was doing a minimum of forty-three miles per hour in a thirty mile an hour speed zone. So she will receive a speeding ticket. About one hundred dollars, I believe."

I am incredulous. "That's *it*? I get to bury my son, and she gets a speeding ticket?"

"I'm afraid that's the law, ma'am. Unfortunately, your son was not in a crosswalk, and Maryland law tends to favor the motorist."

"But this is a school zone!" I sputter angrily. "There's a school across the street. There's a sign that says the speed limit is twenty-five miles per hour."

The detective appears perplexed. "I don't recall seeing that," he admits. "That would change the case considerably. Speeding that much in a school zone would be considered reckless driving. I will check it out."

And check it, he does. But we find that the twenty-five miles per hour limit is only in effect until 4:00 pm. Dov's accident took place at 4:15, when the limit had already changed to thirty.

Later, I ask Tzvi what we should do with the returned items. Like me, he is not sure, he only that he knows he cannot part with them. In the end, I place the bag on a high shelf in Dov's closet, where I know it will be safe, but where I won't have to look at it.

The bag is not the only item that gets stored in Dov's closet. Several weeks after the burial, Rabbi Niman arranges to have Dov's backpack brought to us. Apparently, it had been sitting in his locker all this time. This, unlike the paper bag from the detective, I am curious to open.

I take the backpack up to Dov's room, which still lies untouched: His bed is made, his clothes are folded neatly in his dresser, and his New York Yankees posters still hang on his walls. I open the backpack and take out the first paper I see, an English test, marked with a "92" on it. This was a test he must have just received back. Perhaps he would have shown it to us proudly on the evening of May 31, 2006, if he had only reached the other side of our street safely.

I sit with the test in my hands, remembering how Dov had struggled with English. I think of how switching to the Yeshiva had made such a difference in his life. "Atta boy, Dov," I whisper softly. And then I fold the test in half, close my eyes, and weep.

Chapter 29
Another Accident

"Where's Daddy?" I ask Sarit as I enter the house with Hillel, Noam, and Avichai. We are returning from a nearby pool, one place everybody enjoys going to, even me. The cool water seems to invigorate me and remind me that underneath all the grief I am feeling, there's still some life left in me.

It's been less than a month since Dov died, and as much as I sometimes yearn to do nothing more than curl up in bed and weep, both Tzvi and I are determined to make the summer as normal as possible for our children. Everyone has plans: Hillel, Noam, and Avichai are signed up for day camp, and Sarit is working as a counselor in a different camp for preschoolers.

Before the accident, Tzvi had planned "Camp Daddy," as he called it—a full week of activities with just him and the boys before they started day camp. This is why, three weeks after Dov's funeral, Tzvi takes Hillel, Noam, and Avichai to the Steven F. Udvar-Hazy National Air and Space Museum in Virginia while Sarit and I are at work. They spend another day hiking in the Catoctin Mountains in Maryland, and another day touring a potato chip factory. He snaps pictures of our boys smiling and having fun, with not a hint of grief or pain. Only I know that Tzvi's heart is breaking inside, and I can only guess what my children are feeling. We do our best to keep them busy and maintain some sort of routine, but we know they carry some trauma with them.

This day at the pool is the latest attempt to keep living life as we normally would. The boys drop their wet towels and run upstairs to change into dry clothes, and I turn to Sarit, who has been home for some time. "Daddy did come home, didn't he?"

"Yes, he was out biking, but he's back. But I didn't see him. He just ran upstairs."

Tzvi has recently taken up biking and splurged on a new, pricey bicycle, which he said he would try out today. I run upstairs, eager to hear how it went. And that's when I see that the hall bathroom door is closed. *That's odd.* The boys are in their rooms getting dressed. Tzvi usually uses our master bathroom. Who is in this one?

I knock on the door. "Who is in there?"

"It's me," answers Tzvi. "You can come in. But don't get scared."

I open the door slowly and, oh God, my breath immediately starts coming in short gasps as I take in the scene. Tzvi is sitting on the toilet, holding gauze soaked with blood against his torso, near his groin. There are pools of blood all over the bathroom floor.

"What happened?" I whisper, because I am too scared to talk out loud.

"An accident," he says. "I'm okay. But I am going to need some stitches."

I grab onto the towel rack to steady myself. For a moment, I feel like I might faint. "What kind of accident?" I finally ask, a little more urgently.

"A car ran me off the street. I flipped over my bike and basically impaled myself on my handlebars."

"Oh my God! Where did this happen?"

He pauses. "It happened right down the block. As I was turning from Arcola onto Kemp Mill Road."

"Shit!" I rarely curse, but at this moment in time, I am convinced that no other word will even remotely express the frustration and rage that I am feeling. "*What is going on with our family?* We just buried Dov three weeks ago, and now this! And on our street again!"

"Listen to me," says Tzvi, in a tone that is both calming and commanding. "*I am not going to die.* I need some stitches and that's it. I need you to calm down and help me out here."

"What should I do? Should I call an ambulance?"

"No, I don't need an ambulance. You can just drive me to the Emergency Room."

"Where is the wound?"

He points high on his leg. "It's a deep wound. Would you like to see it?"

I shake my head. "No. Absolutely not. I don't want to see any more blood. Wait here. I need to make some arrangements."

I call Barbara Price and explain the situation. I cannot believe I am asking her for more help, but I'm not sure who else to call. I cannot leave the children alone, and I certainly can't bring them all with us.

Within a moment, she and her daughter Elana are at our door. "Just go," Elana says. "We'll take care of everything."

"You wonderful people," I say. "How did you wind up with such crazy neighbors as us?"

Tzvi wraps his wound and I go to speak to the children. "Daddy hurt himself while biking," I explain, while trying my best to hide my concern. I am determined not to use the word *accident* around them. "We have to see a doctor to get it stitched up. Mrs. Price and Elana will stay with you and give you dinner, and we'll be back as soon as we can."

"Will Daddy be okay?" asks Avichai, and I hear anxiety in his voice.

"I will be *fine*," Tzvi answers from our front hall. "I will be back before you all know it."

I help Tzvi into the car. "Can you drive okay?" he asks. "Because you seem a bit shaken up."

"Of course I'm shaken up. What do you expect? We just buried our son, and now this."

"Yaffa, all I'm asking is, can you drive?"

"I can drive. Please shut up and get in the car."

We head for Holy Cross Hospital, ten minutes from our house, and go straight to the Emergency Room. A triage nurse takes one look at Tzvi's wound and says we will need to wait for a surgeon. Apparently, a few stitches won't do the trick.

I knew it, I think. *Here we go again.*

The nurse sees the worry in my eyes and tries to reassure me. "Don't worry," she says with a smile. "He'll live."

But all I am thinking is, *that's what the social worker told me when we brought Dov in.*

I sit next to Tzvi in our small booth, and we say nothing. I cannot believe that less than three weeks after burying Dov, we are here in the hospital again. But then again, why should I be surprised? Clearly, God has turned His back on us. I certainly can't expect any kind of Divine protection anymore for me or my family. It makes sense: First Dov. Now Tzvi.

And—surprise, surprise—it's an injury close to the groin. Of course. In the depths of despair after Dov's death, I fleetingly thought that maybe—just maybe—we would one day have another child. Here, then, is God's answer: It will never happen. We will be unhappy for the rest of our lives.

Who knows what will happen to Tzvi? They say it can be repaired, but what do they know? There have been cases of people dying inexplicably on the operating table during surgery. Who is to say that will not happen here?

"Yaffa," calls Tzvi, as if reading my thoughts. "They might have to operate on me."

I look at Tzvi. "Yes. They might."

His eyes become wet. "I don't know if I can live through that."

"Yes," I say. "You can."

"No, you don't understand. If I were given the chance to be with Dov..."

"Yes?"

"...I don't think I would want to come back."

I allow a minute for this thought to percolate in my mind. Then I lean close to Tzvi so that my mouth is directly by his ear. "You don't have a *choice*," I whisper fiercely. "Don't you dare leave me. Do you understand? Don't you *dare!*"

He wipes his tears away.

We call my mother-in-law in New York to inform her that we are at the hospital. Again. She tells us to call her whenever we have any news to tell, no matter what the time.

Six hours later, the surgeon comes to check Tzvi's wound. He confirms that Tzvi will need surgery immediately; the wound is quite deep and the doctors need to be sure that there is no internal damage. I begin to shake again. *Here is where it starts*, I think. *They will put him to sleep. And then he will never wake up.*

The nurses wheel him upstairs to prepare him for the operation. He lies stretched out on a gurney while I stand by his side. The nurses question him about allergies, medical complications, and past operations; he responds authoritatively. But when they ask him how he is feeling, he pauses. "I buried my son three weeks ago," he says. "He died after he was hit by a car."

"I'm so sorry," replies the nurse.

"So, I haven't been feeling very good lately."

"Understandable." She looks at me reassuringly. "We'll take good care of him."

It is after midnight when they wheel Tzvi away, and I sit in the lobby with Judy, who has once again come to help, armed with a shopping bag full of food, a siddur, and a great deal of moral support.

"Judy, we have to stop meeting like this."

"This is different," she responds, gripping my arm. "This is not like with Dov. Tzvi will be fine."

I shake my head. I no longer assume that God is on our side. In fact, a part of me mentally prepares for the situation to worsen. The doctor will find internal injuries. Tzvi will become sterile. Or he will slip into a coma during surgery and die. I know that the worst can happen in the blink of an eye.

"Yaffa, really. He will be fine."

"I hope so."

I open the siddur and start to recite Tehillim, which is by now very familiar to me. A part of me wonders, *why are you bothering with this*? But I can't think of any other good option. What else should I do? Sit here and shake like a leaf, imagining the worst? Even if I one day come to the conclusion that prayers are nothing more than a mental relaxation exercise, they still have worth. And a small part of me, I must confess, still holds on to the hope, however ludicrous, that God really listens. That He really does care. That He really watches out for us. Even though it makes no rational sense for me to believe this, it's hard for me to give up this very basic precept.

"Mrs. Klugerman?"

The surgeon has returned, even though Tzvi has been in surgery for less than a half hour. *This is it*, I think, *this is when they tell me that something has gone terribly wrong.*

"Your husband is doing just fine. I repaired the wound and made sure there was no damage inside. It was a very deep wound, but it missed his vital organs by about this much." He holds up his finger and thumb to display an area no bigger than a centimeter.

I exhale deeply. "He's going to be all right?"

"Yes. He'll be sore for some time because we had to go in very deep to repair everything. But he will be fine."

"Oh, thank God. Thank you!"

The relief is overwhelming. I may be a bereaved mother, but for today, at least, I will not be a widow.

"You're welcome," says the doctor. "He's a very lucky man. It seems like someone was looking out for him."

My eyes are wet. "Can I see him?"

"In a little while. He is in recovery now and will be waking up soon."

I give Judy a hug of gratitude and relief. When the nurse beckons to me, I go to see Tzvi. There he is, stretched out on the gurney, looking a bit woozy, but his eyes are open, and he's alive. I stand by his side and take his hand. "Hi there," I say.

"Hey."

"How are you doing?"

"Okay. I think."

My hand is laced in his. "You're going to be okay," I say. "We're going home."

It is well after 1:00 am when we leave the hospital. I call my mother-in-law. "Mom, the surgery is done. Tzvi is okay. We're going home."

"He's okay?" she asks. "Good. Tell him I'm going to *kill* him."

Chapter 30
Virginia Beach

It's been just over a month since Dovie has died, and Tzvi and I have decided that we need to get away.

We are not looking for a romantic vacation; in fact, we are not in the state of mind to even consider anything close to romance, but our lives have been shattered, and somehow we need to figure out how to recalibrate. We have been trying hard to return to our daily routines, but we feel like we are walking through a fog. You can put one step in front of you and make your way from one place to another, but you can't really see beyond that. We lack direction.

Throughout our lives, we have both been drawn to the water, and it is for this reason that we decide to visit Virginia Beach. We have never been there, it's close enough to drive, it's reasonably priced, and—an added bonus—it has a kosher restaurant where we can eat. My parents, who are eager to help in any way they can, agree to drive to Maryland to watch the kids for the two days we will be away. My mother, in particular, understands the importance of this trip and the value of couples taking time for themselves.

"You cannot continue to pour water for your children if your own pitcher is empty," she has always told me.

On the day we depart, we say goodbye to my parents and our children and head south. The trip is just under four hours, and we say little to each other as we make our way farther and farther from our home. We discover that without the regular demands of our life, there's actually not much to say. We aren't discussing what to buy from the supermarket, or who will carpool the kids to their activities. It is just the two of us, alone in our thoughts, carrying a heavy, inescapable burden of grief.

On the first day of our getaway, I realize that I have forgotten to bring flip-flops, but this is no problem; the streets are filled with souvenir stores carrying every type of flip-flop available. I choose a fancier pair with pink stripes and we stroll together past all the shops and food stands. Tzvi poses for a picture in front of a wooden life-size pirate.

"This reminds me of growing up in Atlantic City," I tell him. "It's the beach air. It does something to you."

Although actually, I muse out loud, by the time we were in middle school, my parents tried hard to get us out of the beach atmosphere in which we lived. Every summer, while our neighbors spent entire days at the beach, my siblings and I left to go to camp. And once we were older, the whole family spent summers at a bungalow colony in upstate New York.

"Why didn't you just stay home?" Tzvi asks. "I grew up on the beach in Brooklyn. We belonged to a beach club. That's what we did every summer."

"My father didn't like that people were basically walking around everywhere in their underwear," I explain. "It's the beach mentality. It loosens the morals. He wanted to get us away from that."

We pick a spot on the beach and spread out a blanket. The salty air hits my nostrils and I breathe deeply. I lie down and close my eyes. Slowly, the horror and pain I've been feeling are temporarily calmed and moved to the side. For the first time in weeks, I feel a sense of peace.

I realize that nobody on the beach knows who we are and what we have been through. We look like a normal couple out for a day on the beach. The anonymous, carefree husband and wife. That's us. It makes me want to laugh. And then another thought pops into my head: What about the people surrounding us? What pains do they carry that we cannot see? I scrutinize the families holding hands in the ocean, the children digging dams in the sand. They look perfectly natural and normal. But I know now that it's possible, in fact probable, that many carry with them some sort of pain as well. Nothing is as it appears to be.

We stand and move toward the ocean. The water is perfect, and Tzvi and I stand hand in hand as the surf repeatedly covers our toes and then pulls back. Again, I inhale deeply. I discover that there is something uniquely therapeutic about being on a beach. It's something that gives me a hint of hope that perhaps, someday, the pain won't hurt as much.

Tzvi and I don't talk much, and we experience ups and downs. We enjoy going out to eat at the small kosher restaurant, and later we walk together on the beach as the sun sets. It's a romantic setting, even if we are not in the mood for romance, and it's easy to appreciate and savor where we are. But we can only keep the pain at bay for so long. That night, we weep together in our hotel room.

On our second and last day at Virginia Beach, we swim together until our fingers and toes are wrinkled. I feel my nose burning and reach for the suntan lotion. I inhale deeply and turn to Tzvi, because the strangest thought has suddenly popped into my head.

"Tzvi," I say, "I think we should have another child."

He just looks at me.

Chapter 31
Losing Faith

Our tradition tells a story about Elisha ben Avuya, who was one of the great sages of the Talmud. One day he spied a young boy climbing a ladder set against a tree; the boy was performing the commandment of chasing a mother bird from her nest before removing her eggs. The commandment is reputed to demonstrate great mercy; rather than forcing the mother bird to witness her young being snatched away, we send her elsewhere. So significant is this commandment, that the Torah notes that those who observe it are guaranteed long lives. But Elisha ben Avuya observed this young boy carefully shoo away the mother bird and remove her eggs—and then lose his balance and fall to his death. Unable to come to terms with what he witnessed, Elisha ben Avuya concluded that God did not exist and rejected his faith entirely. His opinions are found throughout the Talmud, and the sages do not remove his words, but they refuse to use his name any longer. Instead, he is referred to as *Acher*—the other.

Acher and me. We could be buddies. I don't agree with him, but so help me, I certainly understand him. How else does one explain a world in which injustice occurs except by concluding that a just God does not exist? My son was learning Torah in a Yeshiva. He crossed a street to come home. He lost his life in the tiny space between the two locales in which he felt the safest. How does one explain such a horrific turn of events?

162 | THE BROKEN VASE

On the outside, I am perceived as a woman with tremendous faith in God. But on the inside, I now carry with me a deep, dark secret: I question it all.

My faith is like a precious gem, locked safely in a secure vault, whose value I have always presumed to be real. Now, I demand the key, determined to hold and examine this fabled stone with my own eyes. Are there flaws? Is it cracked? Is it genuine? I must find out. For if it is not real, then neither is my life.

Once upon a time, I believed that God had a plan. I believed that if one looked hard enough, one was bound to see divine providence everywhere: in nature; in life; and yes, even in death. But now I know the truth: It is easy to maintain one's faith when things are good. A little pain can challenge that faith. A lot of pain can obliterate any trace of it, and make you realize how naïve and foolish you were to believe in any kind of divine plan.

For the first time in my life, I am forced to grapple with a question whose answer I had always previously took for granted: Does God exist?

Perhaps, I think, my entire life is a lie. Maybe there is no purpose to keeping Shabbat, eating kosher food, and immersing myself in a mikvah. Perhaps, when I pray, nobody listens. Perhaps this is all one large, elaborate fabrication designed to give us the security of believing that there is order in the world, and a purpose to our lives. Perhaps there is no God. Perhaps the world was created by accident, the result of some rare chemical reaction that created life. Perhaps we human beings are here wholly by coincidence, as random combinations of DNA, and after we die, we will be gone forever.

It's possible. I wouldn't have even considered it before, but Dov being killed shakes up the way I view everything. Did the accident occur because there is no God? Did it happen because, in truth, there is nobody in charge looking out for our children, and we live in a world of chaos, where anything at all can happen?

"What if you found out today that you weren't actually Jewish?" I ask Tzvi. "What if there was some sort of mixup at the hospital or something, and it turns out that you're not a Jew? What would you do?"

Tzvi doesn't hesitate. "I would convert."

"Immediately?"

"Well, of course." But I can see that he is thinking it over. "Actually, maybe I would wait a bit. Maybe I would go out and try a cheeseburger first."

"And then you would convert?"

"You know," he says, as he turns the theoretical question over in his head, "I'm not sure. Maybe I would take a few months and go travel without having to worry about Shabbat or finding kosher food. Maybe I would just go see the world first, and then I would come back and convert."

"So let me get this straight. You leave your family, your job, your siddur and tefillin for a few months, and go and see the world? Wouldn't it be strange for you to be traveling on Shabbat? You would be able to completely leave your Jewish life behind while you experience life as a non-Jew?"

"I don't know. If I were single, I would do it in a second. But I guess it wouldn't be so easy to just leave everything like that. I would have to think about it."

It wasn't the first time we had discussed this. Often, while traveling, we would stop at rest stops and marvel at how "ordinary people" could simply buy meals wherever they found themselves, without thinking twice, while we had to pack everything up in advance. At rest stops; in malls and movie theaters; in whatever city, town, or village they find themselves in, most people can just buy food whenever they feel hungry. *The goyim*, we would say, *have no idea how easy they have it.*

I try to grasp the notion of going to movies on Friday nights, and watching Saturday morning cartoons. I imagine what it would be like to attend a weekend beach party dressed in a skimpy bikini, playing volleyball with men, and eating hamburgers and ice cream at the same meal. It's a world I've never tasted before, and here is my opportunity to experience it. I could renounce God and give everything up: I could change my name, my dress, and my entire lifestyle. My family and friends would be saddened, no doubt, but nobody would blame me. *Poor woman*, they would say. *Her son died in a tragic accident and she lost her faith.*

But I realize that I have a lot to lose if I give up God. All of Judaism is based on the one basic, simple belief that a Creator exists. My communal life, my family life, are built around that belief. If I decide not to believe in God, I stand to lose it all—my community, my family, and a good part of myself. It's an enormous price to pay for losing one's faith.

I also concede that the idea of having so much freedom terrifies me. I truly cannot imagine a week without Shabbat. I cannot conceive of eating a meat meal served with a glass of milk. I cannot bear to think of the loneliness and horror of living in a world completely alone, without my family, my community, and my people. Still, I realize that I cannot live the life I lead unless I absolutely believe that what I am doing is correct. As terrifying as it might be to live in a world without God, it is far better than continuing to live a lie. And so, I am forced to confront the question honestly, because I cannot continue with my life if it is left unanswered.

Do I believe in God?

I ponder these thoughts for months, even as I continue to go through the motions of leading an observant lifestyle. I eat my kosher food, I light my Shabbat candles, and I dutifully play the part of the religious wife and mother, even though, inside my mind, everything is bedlam.

At some point, I find my answer, and it is resounding.

I do believe.

Not because I feel God's presence. Feelings are often irrational, and to answer this question, I require a purely rational answer. I realize that it simply doesn't make sense to me that human beings should exist unless some higher power created us. Great order exists in nature, and I believe that a natural, unguided world would be chaos. Great symphonies don't simply come into being; someone must put thousands of disparate notes together and create harmony. Great works of literature don't write themselves; someone organizes thoughts and uses words to put them on paper. Even within the four walls of my own house, there is a symphony of sorts, but socks don't sort themselves; someone must tidy and clean to keep things in order. So, it stands to reason that our Earth would not necessarily orbit the sun and our hearts would not necessarily beat—unless some Being had designed them to do so.

So yes, I believe in God, and though I grapple with the question, I do not hesitate with my answer. Maybe we could be buddies, but I am not *Acher*. I am absolutely sure that God exists.

This, however, leaves me with a much more troubling question: If God exists, what is His role in this world? Where was He on the day Dov crossed the street? Does He just sit back and allow disastrous things to happen to unsuspecting people? The more I contemplate this, the more I believe that most people do not need to be convinced of God's existence. The more debatable question is: To what degree is God involved in our lives?

I know that the questions I am asking are not new. Lethal accidents happen regularly. Disease is rampant. Children die every day. Jewish history is replete with horrific events like the Spanish Inquisition, the Holocaust, and terror attacks in Israel. Why would I think that I was immune? And the answer, if I'm honest, is that I was blissfully naïve. I could accept that terrible things happened, but I never expected that something so awful would ever happen to *me*.

Some would say that God allows the world to run on its own, and He doesn't interfere. Jewish tradition rejects this notion entirely. Every day we proclaim in our prayers, "He who illuminates the earth…and in His goodness renews daily, always, the work of creation." We believe that if God was not around to turn the Earth and make the sun rise every day, then it simply would not happen. We believe God is perpetually involved in creation.

And I do believe God is involved with our lives—certainly at least to some extent. In my career, I've worked with donors, and I've never met any who simply give a cause their money and leave. No, if they invest in a cause, then they might not be included in every single task, but they do demand to be involved in some way. It does not make sense to me that God would go to the trouble of creating an entire world and then just let it completely run itself. I am certain that He is still very much involved, although I understand why some might find it easier to love a God who is powerless to stop tragedy than one who allows it to happen, or even, for whatever unfathomable reason, orchestrates it Himself.

But, asks that deep inner voice, *if God is still running the world, then why did Dov die?*

This is the question that haunts me. If I give God credit for bringing Dov into this world, then intellectual honesty demands that I acknowledge His role in removing Dov from this world. I must accept that God was *not* sleeping the day of Dov's accident. God was there, and for whatever reason, this was part of His plan. I am forced to acquaint myself with the God whom few of us recognize; the God who not only rescues a crew from an airplane crash, but caused the airplane motors to accidentally shut down in the first place. The same God is responsible for life and death, good and evil, the miraculous and the tragic. This God is a far cry from the benevolent, kind, merciful God I grew up with. And like it or not, He is the God I must somehow come to terms with if I am to continue living my life as an observant Jew. For just as I am certain that God exists, I am also quite sure that He is the only one.

I realize that most of the world only sees and acknowledges God when something good occurs. One day, I hear on the news that a bridge has collapsed without warning. As a result, many people tragically die. But I see a woman who points to a school bus full of children who were unharmed, and calls it a miracle.

What about the rest of the people who died? I think. *Why couldn't God save them all? And if God did save the school bus, then who, exactly, caused the bridge to collapse?*

I wonder who is responsible for God's brilliant PR. Just how is it that He gets credit for the good, but is blameless for the bad?

"I have come to the conclusion," I tell Tzvi, "that the relationship we have with God is an abusive one."

Tzvi eyes me warily and chuckles. "That's certainly an interesting observation. What do you mean, exactly?"

I pause to think of an appropriate example. "Well, you're an educator," I reply. "Imagine for a moment that one of your students has a close relationship with her father. The father, as a gift, gives the child a dog, which she adores."

Tzvi is listening. "Go on."

"One day, with no explanation, the father takes a shotgun and kills the dog. The child cannot understand what has happened. She approaches her father, crying, and asks why he has killed her beloved pet. And the father says...nothing at all.

"This child is your student. Would you not consider the father to be abusive? Wouldn't you report him? What kind of twisted relationship is it when a father knowingly hurts a child, and won't even explain why?

"And now, imagine for a moment that it isn't a child, but an adult; and it isn't a dog, but a son. Don't you think, at the very least, God owes us an explanation? What in the world did we do to deserve this pain?"

"Yaffa, God is not a father."

"In our prayers, we refer to Him as our father."

"But God is not a human being. We don't see situations the way God sees them. He sees the entire picture, and our sight is limited."

"I think that's a lame answer."

"Maybe," he says, looking me in the eye, "but we have no other."

I expect to cry, but there are no tears, only anger. I am entirely dissatisfied, and there is absolutely no court of appeals which will hear my case, and no customer service representative to whom I can complain. And in that moment, I realize I have lost far more than my son; I have also lost the God I once loved. Gone is the God I turned to my entire life, expecting Him to love me and protect me. And in His place is an implacable, unknowable entity capable of inflicting unbearable and unwarranted pain.

Chapter 32
Miracles

I replay the accident hundreds of times a day. Each time, I think of all the factors that allowed it to take place, and how changing one of those factors even slightly would have altered the outcome.

If only Dov hadn't been enrolled at the Yeshiva, the accident would not have occurred. He would have been safe and sound, learning at the Melvin J. Berman Hebrew Academy in Rockville, as he had been since kindergarten. He switched to the Yeshiva only three months before he died.

If only we didn't live on Arcola Avenue, the accident would not have occurred. Dov would have remained in school during his afternoon break, as his classmates did. Only because we lived so close to the Yeshiva did he even consider coming home.

If only Dov hadn't chosen to come home for a break, the accident would not have occurred. He did not need to cross the street at that time. He could have simply used the bathroom at school and eaten his snack there. No compelling reason had forced him to cross at that moment in time.

If only the driver had been abiding by the speed limit, the accident would not have occurred. The driver was determined to have been traveling at a speed of at least forty-three miles per hour. At a slower speed, she could have stopped in time, or Dov could have crossed in time. Members of our community gather to discuss pedestrian safety on Arcola Avenue. They point out that had there been two lanes, instead of four, or if there had been a pedestrian island in the center of the road, Dov would have been able to cross safely.

The detective told us that the entire event took place within two seconds. I wonder: what if someone at school had detained Dovie for just three seconds? What if a teacher or friend had wanted to ask him a question or tell him something? What if I had been outside, and screamed at him not to cross the street? What if his shoe had been untied, and he had crouched down to tie it before he crossed?

How many factors had to be lined up just so, for the tragedy to happen as it did? What were the chances that such a horrific incident would actually take place?

My mother-in-law cries that she could have prevented the accident if only she had told Dov to be more careful crossing the street. My mother confesses that she missed reciting her daily Tehillim that morning; if only she had said them, she is certain the accident would not have occurred. Tzvi is convinced that if only he had been present at the scene, he would have been able to save Dov. It seems that almost everyone is ready to take the blame for Dov's accident. Judy confesses to me that she feels guilty that she ever told me it was a good idea to buy our house. The Hebrew Academy school bus driver asks for Tzvi's forgiveness; he often dropped Noam and Avichai at our house at precisely the time that Dov would take his afternoon break, and Dov would take advantage of the traffic halting to cross the street safely. But on the day of the accident, the bus arrived at our house early. If only I had arrived later, says the bus driver, in tears, Dov would be alive today.

I think about all these scenarios. I begin to believe that if I can change the scenario so easily in my head, I should have been able to change the actual outcome. I think of dozens of ways that the accident could have been easily avoided. But I begin to realize that, just as I tried to do as a child, I am piecing together a broken vase. No matter how much glue I use to try and put it together, it will always be hopelessly cracked. Nevertheless, I continue to mull over the accident, because I cannot believe it happened. I simply cannot believe it happened.

What were the chances? I think. *Really,* what *were the chances?*

I discover that in Montgomery County, Maryland, home to over 930,000 residents, more than 430 pedestrians have been struck by vehicles so far this year. Of those 430, seventeen, including Dov, were killed. If the statistics are correct, then the chances of being struck by a vehicle at all are less than half of one percent. The chances of being hit and *killed* by a vehicle are less than one-thousandth of one percent. If we were talking about something with a positive outcome, then I would most assuredly have called it a miracle.

I even know of one.

It was a sticky summer day in Brooklyn. A mother placed her baby in the carriage, ready to run some errands. She fanned her face with her hand, trying and failing to find some relief from the heat before setting out down the busy street. She was trudging slowly when a passing breeze caught her by surprise. Perhaps, she worried, it wasn't as warm as she'd thought. Instinctively, she lifted the hood of the carriage, shielding her baby from the cool air, and continued on her way. The baby was lulled to sleep by the movement, and soon the mother returned to their apartment, carrying the carriage with the sleeping baby up a flight of stairs, and parking it outside her front door.

She had just gone inside the apartment to get a cool glass of water when she heard a loud crash. She rushed back out only to discover that the carriage was no longer by the door. She was panic stricken when she saw it at the foot of the steps, upside down, its wheels turning in the air. There was no sound coming from the carriage.

She raced down the steps, her horror mounting with each stride. Why wasn't the baby crying? Kneeling by the fallen carriage, she discovered her daughter curled up in its hood, still sleeping peacefully.

"That baby was you," my mother would tell me, many times. "And that breeze was a miracle."

Where was that breeze, God, when my son was about to cross the street to his death? A breeze might have swept his yarmulke off his head, and he would have paused to retrieve it! A breeze might have blown dust in his eyes, and he could have stopped to rub them! A breeze might have rushed pollen up his nose, and he may have stopped in his tracks to sneeze. Why did I get a breeze, but my son didn't?

Just a few seconds, Lord. That's all that was needed to save his life.

Dov's death turns everything I have ever heard about miraculous events upside down. Now, when I think about the passing breeze that made my mother lift my carriage hood on a warm summer day, saving me from certain injury and perhaps even death, I wonder: *If God sent the breeze, then who pushed the carriage down the steps?*

Chapter 33
Grief Therapy

The small office has a homey feel to it. I am the only one sitting in the waiting room, looking through vacuous magazines for women, and hardly hearing the background music. Karen Prince has been recommended to me as an excellent grief therapist, which is good, because I could use some excellent grief therapy right about now.

She emerges from a back room—a smiling, petite woman, wearing glasses, with a knowing look that somehow conveys that she has seen it all. I like her immediately. She leads me into another room, where I sit down right next to a fresh box of tissues.

After a bit of prompting, I tell her my story. I talk about seeing Dov injured right in front of my house. I tell her about the nine long days in the hospital, and how people cared for us. I speak about waking up in the morning and not wanting to get out of bed. About how I cannot see myself ever living a happy life again. I talk about worrying for my husband and children. I am afraid we will never recover.

I've told this story so many times that I'm not actually crying, but she is. As the minutes pass, she grabs one tissue after another and dabs her eyes as she listens.

She is an excellent listener. She waits until I'm finished before she speaks. "I had heard about your son," she says. "It's a terrible story. I'm so sorry for your loss."

"Thank you."

"You've experienced a horrific tragedy. You have every reason to feel the way you do. But if you don't figure out how to go on with your life, then you will have five more tragedies on your hands."

"Five more?" I ask.

"Five. Your husband and your four children. All of their lives will be tragic if you cannot figure out how to deal with this terrible grief."

I digest these words carefully. *Five tragedies.* Never mind the earthquake; it's the aftershocks that can apparently do the most damage. "I don't know how to do it," I admit. "I don't think I can ever be happy again."

"That is why you are here. And that is what we are going to work on."

Every week, we meet for an hour. I talk. We cry. We replace the box of tissues. I do not feel better, but I begin to appreciate the opportunity to weep at a designated time every week. Structured grief. That's what these sessions offer me. And it's effective, because my life feels like a mess, and any control over it offers some degree of comfort. It's like I have a storage box to hold my pain during the week, where it can be saved and contained, and then I can open it and feel it properly during one of my grief sessions.

It also gives me the chance to vent. I talk about the stupid things that people sometimes say to me, and Karen agrees and empathizes. I talk about how guilty I feel about the accident.

"It could have happened anywhere," she says.

"But we live on a busy street! He would have been safer on a quieter street. I should have never agreed to buy that house."

"It happens on quiet streets, too."

"But it happens less!"

She sits, listens, nods, and shows me the flaws in the ways I am thinking. I don't buy everything she tells me, but it is good to talk to someone who will let me say what I want to say.

I tell her I can't stop thinking of how Dov must feel about being killed.

"What do you think he feels?"

"In my mind, I keep seeing him," I say. "He's waving his fists and screaming, 'It's not fair! It's not fair!'"

"We're going to change that image right now. From now on, when you think of Dov, I want you to try your best to think of him as being happy and content."

"He can't be happy and content," I snap. "He was killed before he even turned fifteen!"

But still, I see her point. It's tough to get on with your life when you picture your dead child consumed with anger. Somehow, I have to figure out how to change my perspective.

"Tell me a story about Dov," Karen says. "A happy story."

And so I tell her about something that happened about a week before his accident. That was when I almost hit a pedestrian.

Dov was sitting in the front seat of our car, next to me, while two of his Yeshiva cronies sat in the back. We were on our way to the Regal Majestic movie theater, where they were planning to see the latest *X-Men* movie, when an ambulance cut us off from the opposite direction. Stuck in the crosswalk as the light turned green, I tried to back up to allow pedestrians to cross—but I didn't see a woman darting behind my car as I tried to back up.

Fortunately, Dov did, and yelled to stop. I slammed on the brakes just in time.

"Where in the world did she come from?" I asked, a bit shaken up.

Dov just shook his head. "I can't believe you did that."

I ignored him. "Now," I said, when we pulled up at the movie theater, "just remember what I told you."

"I know, I know. We need to get the tickets and go straight into the theater."

I hadn't been thrilled about letting Dovie go to the movie, but I had given in to his pleas. "This isn't the greatest area," I noted. "Don't hang around, okay? No playing video games. Just buy your tickets and go in."

"Mom, I know. We've been through this."

"The movie should start in about fifteen minutes, so you're here just in time."

"Fine." He hopped out of the car with his friends, exhibiting the typical teenage leave-me-alone-I-want-my-independence attitude. But I caught his smile.

"Have a good time."

"Thanks, Mom."

Five minutes later, as I was making my way home, my cell phone rang.

"Mom?"

"Yes, Dovie. Everything okay?"

"The movie is sold out. The next show is in a half hour. What do you want me to do?"

Most teens would have simply bought tickets to the next show without thinking twice, but I had made it clear that I wanted Dov and his friends to go straight into the theater. Since that was impossible, he called. I knew that he expected me to say that I would be right there to pick them up and bring them home. After all, in his mind, I was the Ultra-Cautious Mother: I forbade him from watching R-rated movies or playing M-rated video games; I installed Internet controls on his computer; I hesitated before allowing him to go skiing. It stood to reason that I would have objections to him hanging out waiting for a half hour in an area I wasn't so comfortable about.

"All right, Dovie," I finally said. "Buy the tickets to the next movie. And then just wait there until you can go in."

"You said this is not a good area."

"It's not," I agreed.

"And that you don't want me hanging around the theater."

"I don't," I replied, "but you'll be all right. I trust you."

I couldn't see his face, but I knew he was smiling. "Mom, thank you."

I caught a glimpse of him as he arrived home later that evening, dropped off by his friend's mother. His face shone with... what was it, exactly? Pride? Happiness? Freedom? Whatever it was, it looked wonderful.

"How was the movie?" I asked.

"Awesome."

"Any problems?"

"Nope."

"Great. Glad you enjoyed."

Later that week, I held his hand in the hospital as he lay there, unconscious, and again and again, I remembered that carefree evening; how Dov checked with me before purchasing tickets, and the joy I heard in his voice after I placed my nerves on hold and allowed him to be a teenager. The smile on his face when he got home.

I had had no idea that movie would be his last. I couldn't have imagined how little time he had left. Perhaps, in retrospect, the close call with the pedestrian was another omen of what was to come. But I grabbed hold of that memory and considered how an ordinary evening out turned out to be an event of such significance.

"I'm so glad," I tell Karen, "that I let him go to that movie."

Days after this conversation, I read a legendary story about Itzhak Perlman, who once broke a string on his violin during a concert but continued to play magnificently. When he finished, he turned to the audience and said, "Sometimes, it is our task to find out how much music we can make with what we have left."

This must be my goal, I think. Finding the music in what we have left. My family will never be what it was, not without Dovie, but perhaps there is some way to create something new. I print the sentence out and hang it inside my most-used kitchen cabinet, so that I can be reminded of it every day.

Chapter 34
Philadelphia

Bikur Cholim of Greater Washington has been an incredible help to our family since Dovie's accident. Having provided meals and moral support throughout Dovie's hospitalization, they have continued checking in with us constantly, to see how they can assist.

Audrey Siegel, executive director of BCGW, reaches out to me with another generous offer. "Many people made donations to Bikur Cholim of Greater Washington while Dovie was in the hospital, and later, in his memory," she tells me. "We think the money should be used to help your family in some way. Tell me what we can do for you."

Tzvi and I come up with an answer almost immediately. The trip to Virginia Beach helped us as a couple. A family vacation would undoubtedly benefit us all as well. Could BCGW help us pay for a trip?

Audrey is only too happy to agree, and we begin to make plans. In no time, we settle on Philadelphia, where we hope to visit some historical sites with the kids. Perhaps we will also spend a day at the beach near where I grew up in Margate, New Jersey.

And so, at the beginning of August, just two months after Dovie's death, the six of us pack up our van and head to Philadelphia. It will be our first family vacation without Dovie. I find myself wondering, how will we do it? Or, more to the point, how will I go touring without bursting into tears at every site, thinking of how Dovie would have loved it?

When you're grieving, there's a first time for everything. Going to the supermarket and not buying the foods Dovie loved was excruciating the first time I did it. Visiting his school to pick up some papers—a truly awful experience. Even taking the kids to the dentist without Dovie brought me to tears. But here's the thing: I find that once I do it, I realize that I can do it again. The pain is not completely gone the second time around, but it has lessened somewhat. It's more bearable. I realize that at some point I have to figure out how to have fun with my kids while knowing that one will always be missing. And I also have to show them that they can still experience joy, even if they've lost a beloved brother. I know that if I can't succeed with that, then all my children will suffer.

So, during our vacation, I put on a happy face. I try to be excited about visiting the Liberty Bell, even when the kids (rightfully) complain that it's boring, and Avichai decides to lie down on the floor of Independence Hall and go to sleep while the tour guide is speaking. We visit the Franklin Institute and check out the exhibits. We go on the duck tour, which travels on land and water, and I smile and point at the sights.

I try. I really do. But inside, my heart is breaking.

We check into our hotel, which is lovely, and contains a small kitchen so we can prepare our meals. We go swimming in the pool on the roof. We smile for pictures. We do everything that normal families would do on a family vacation. The pain is there, as it always is. But we do our very best to work around it.

On the second day, we tour Philadelphia some more and then head to a kosher Chinese restaurant in Bala Cynwyd for dinner. An old friend of ours manages the place, and he comes out to greet us. He and Tzvi shake hands. He has heard, of course—is there anybody who hasn't heard?—and offers his condolences.

We order our dinner, and the food is delicious. When we finish, the manager tells us that the meal is on the house. "It's the very least I can do for you," he says, with tears in his eyes.

This is the effect we have on people. They realize there is nothing they can do to change the grief and loss we will face every day of our lives, so they offer their small tokens of friendship to keep us going. They cook meals. They do our laundry. They carpool our children. They fund our vacation. They cannot erase the grief, but for several moments in time, they can do something to help ease the pain. The gestures may seem small to them, in the grand scheme of things, but we appreciate and remember every single one.

The next day, we head to the Jersey Shore to take the kids to the beach. This is the best day of all. It is the first time that four-year-old Avichai has seen the ocean. He is amazed and delighted, and I snap one picture after another of him gathering shells, building sandcastles, and frolicking in the water. For me, it's a return to the beach life of Margate, New Jersey, the place where I grew up. I am reminded of warm summer nights inhaling the scent of the beach, of houses with outdoor showers for washing off sand, of biking on the boardwalk. It's a step back in time, to when my life was far more simple, and simply happy, than it is today.

The beach has the same therapeutic effect on the children as it did on me and Tzvi at Virginia Beach. We jump over waves and relax on our towels. We apply and reapply sunscreen, but we burn anyway, and we don't care. Despite all that has transpired in the past two months, we succeed in having a truly fun day.

Dovie would have loved this, I think, again, but then I push the thought away, the way I have been doing throughout the trip.

Chapter 35
Bereaved Parents

I receive a phone call from someone named Esther Nitzlich. As it turns out, I find out that she is my father's cousin, which makes us first cousins once removed.

I'm not surprised to hear from distant relatives. The truth is that I have literally hundreds of cousins whom I've never met. My paternal grandfather Moshe was one of ten siblings. Three of them were murdered during the Holocaust. The other seven, including him, left Europe to immigrate to the United States. Their descendants live all over the world, and I've only met a small percentage of them.

Esther calls me because, like many others, she has heard what has happened. And because, as it turns out, she knows exactly how I feel. "We lost our son the same way," she says. "He was crossing the street and was hit by a truck."

She tells me more about the incident; how her son, if he had lived, would be an adult now, probably with children of his own. How she went on to give birth to many more children, but never forgot the one she lost. She knows how hard it is, she tells me. "You have my number," she says. "Call me anytime."

I am deeply moved by the call. Here is someone I have never met in my life, reaching out to me because we have shared a devastating experience. I take a lot of comfort in knowing that there are other people who have gone through what we are going through, and have moved forward.

Many weeks later, after a particularly difficult Shabbat, when guilty thoughts were getting the best of me, I decide to take Esther up on her offer. It's about 10 pm, but I need to speak to someone who understands what I'm going through. And she had said to call anytime. So, with some nervousness, I call.

"Shavua tov, this is Yaffa Klugerman. Remember me? I'm the cousin you called a few weeks ago."

"Of course," she says. "*Gut voch*. How are you?"

"I have a question, and I was hoping you could answer it. I know it's late, but I feel like you are one of the only people I know who can answer this honestly."

"I'll do my best."

"The question is this," I say. "Did you ever feel like it was your fault that your son was killed? Like what happened was a punishment? Because I can't stop thinking that way. I keep thinking that I must have done something wrong."

There's a long pause on the other end. "No," she says, "I don't think I could live with myself if I thought that what happened was a punishment."

"But then," I ask, "why do these things happen?"

"Who understands these terrible *nisyonos*?" she replies. "Nobody does. Nobody. Just a minute, my husband is standing right here and he wants to speak to you."

She hands the phone to her husband, who immediately begins to speak to me, this person whom he's never met, but can understand intimately.

He tells me a story of a great rabbi who dies tragically. His community, his family, his students cannot understand how God allowed such a terrible thing to occur. Until one learned man explained that that is the way God works. His ways are complex and hidden and are not supposed to be understood. "Do you understand?" Esther's husband says. "There's no way to understand these terrible things. God has His own plans. We just have to keep believing."

The two of them stay on the phone with me for a full hour, encouraging me and offering their words of wisdom, until I feel like I can go on without blaming myself. I carry their words with me for a long time.

Esther is one of the first bereaved parents I talk to, but she is by no means the last. The death of my son qualifies me to be a part of, as many call it, "the club nobody wants to join." I learn about grief support groups and email groups for bereaved parents. It's as if an entire population of people that I've never noticed before has suddenly come to life before my eyes. I learn that many, many parents have lost children, and that we share many of the same emotions.

I join a grieving parents' email listserv group, where I discover pretty quickly that I'm not alone in how I am feeling. One mother, whose son died at age seventeen, shares the following:

> I will tell you that the first year is a year that is filled with hard, gut-wrenching anguish.... Some days are mind boggling...some days I felt numb. Some days I felt like I could not take the next breath. Honestly, there were those days that I would wake up from a sleep and wonder why I was in so much pain...and then the full realization would hit me like a ton of bricks once again. There were days that I would drive to and from work and bawl my eyes out the entire time. There were days that I would cry in the office and in traffic. I cried multiple times every single day. There were and still are days that I open my moon roof in my car and scream at the top of my lungs. There are days that I took a wiffle ball bat and beat a tree. There were days that I would take celery stalks and beat them against a table because I liked to hear the splintering sound. There was a day that I dropped a large picture frame and the glass bust into thousands of shards...I sat there looking at the glass and thinking that my life was like those thousand shards...

184 | THE BROKEN VASE

never to be put back together. I picked up those pieces
of glass until my hands were bleeding, and I didn't care.

From this listserv, I find out that the aftermath of a sudden
traumatic death can be worse than the incident itself. People tell
of divorces, of children taking drugs, of suicides, of never recover-
ing. The horror that might be in store for our family is too much
to handle. I decide that I've read enough, and I leave the group.

But then a bereaved parent who lives in my community
tells me of a smaller email group for Jewish bereaved parents,
and I agree to give it a try. There are perhaps thirty parents in
all, but there we can talk about Jewishly themed death subjects,
like reciting Kaddish and Yizkor, and finding the right wording
for a tombstone. We can also talk about how we can go on
believing in God after experiencing what we have. There is no
judgment in the group, and you can say whatever you want,
which is refreshing.

I join the group in August 2006, and this is how I introduce
myself:

> Hello all, and I'm sorry we're meeting under such
> unhappy circumstances.
>
> My name is Yaffa, and I just buried my oldest son
> Dov, age fourteen, about two months ago. Our house
> is located directly across from his school, and he was
> crossing the street to our house while on a break from
> classes when he was struck by a speeding SUV. He was
> an incredibly responsible, careful kid, and had crossed
> that street safely hundreds of times before, so we can
> only surmise that either he didn't see the vehicle com-
> ing, or that he didn't realize how fast she was traveling.
> Mercifully, I did not see the accident, but I was home at
> the time, so I stayed with him and talked to him while
> he lay unconscious and bleeding in the middle of the
> street, and accompanied him in the ambulance.

At the hospital, we were shocked to be told that Dov had suffered massive brain injuries, and that he very likely would not survive the night. Miraculously, his condition improved in the beginning, and he remained alive for nine very difficult days. During that time, our family, friends, community, and even people we'd never met prayed for him and supported us in every imaginable way. But his condition started deteriorating, and he passed away on June 8.

We have four other children, ages four to thirteen. We are going on with our lives as best as we can, and people have been incredibly supportive, but the grief hits us at different times and the pain can be unbelievable. It's so hard to believe that we had a beautiful, healthy child, with plans for camp and the future, and in one second everything changed, and our lives were shattered forever.

I would be grateful to hear from anyone who has been down this horrific road before. Can anyone really recover from the loss of a child? I can't imagine that the pain ever completely goes away.

Gratefully,

Yaffa Klugerman

The responses come quickly.

"Our daughter was diagnosed with a brain tumor and died at age thirteen..."

"My son died from leukemia..."

"We lost our fourteen-year-old to a genetic disease that has killed several generations in my husband's family."

One mother writes that her son was hit by a van in front of her house while riding a scooter. I write her back almost immediately with questions. Did they move to another house? Did they live on a busy street? She tells me that they had just moved into the house two months prior to the accident, so they felt guilty that maybe they shouldn't have bought that house. But they stayed for some years, until eventually moving out.

Everyone offers advice. Another mother says:

> "It" (the grief, the pain, the anger, the despair, the overwhelming emptiness) changes, but stays with you. The other day I was pushing a cart through the parking lot of the grocery store and my head started spinning. It felt like lead. It hit me like a ton of bricks. My son was dead. What did I do? Got in my car, went home and made dinner.
>
> It is my experience that yes, you can recover. But not in the way most people think. I found that I will never, ever go back to that carefree, innocent young mom I was. I get a lot of inspiration from Holocaust survivors. They went through this horrible experience, picked themselves off, and went on to have new lives with new families. The pain is not totally gone. It lurks deep inside, waiting for the right (or wrong, depending how you look at it) moment. But I have laughed and enjoyed myself, which I thought would never, ever happen again.

What is striking to me is that many of the parents on this email group lost their children years ago, yet they still find it beneficial to share experiences and vent to people who understand them. The pain gets easier with time, they say, but it never goes away completely.

I begin to understand that there's really no one way to "get through" the loss of a child; in fact, it's not really about getting through it at all. It's about acknowledging that life has changed irreversibly, and figuring out how to go on in spite of that. To do that, you look for support wherever you can find it, and one of the best places to find that support is with other bereaved parents.

As one mother tells me:

I think that when others see those who are still functioning after such a tragedy, it helps them know that they can go on too. Somehow knowing you are not the only one helps just a little.

Chapter 36
The Question

Tzvi and I travel to attend the wedding of my dear friend Baila. She and her fiancé, Danny, are about my age and are getting married for the first time.

Baila and I have been friends for nearly thirty years. I met her in summer camp when we were only eleven and, incredibly, we have kept in touch ever since. Ours is the type of friendship that we have always been able to pick up again, even if we haven't spoken for months. Which is why her wedding is an event that both Tzvi and I are thrilled to attend.

But it is the first real social event we experience as bereaved parents. It also marks the first time that I experience what will become a lifelong struggle for me: how to respond when someone asks me how many children I have.

It happens with no warning. I am seated at a table with Cindi, and we meet an acquaintance from camp whom we haven't seen for decades. We exchange small talk, and soon enough, she asks the question.

I hesitate. "Four," I answer quietly.

Cindi is watching me closely. She knows exactly what is going on, and all the horror that stands behind my one syllable reply.

"Boys or girls?"

"One girl," I say, unable to look her in the eye. "Three boys."

"Is she the oldest?"

Again, I hesitate. Dovie was the oldest. How to answer this seemingly innocuous question that picks at such deep, recent wounds? Cindi looks at me knowingly. Neither of us knows what to do. "Yes."

"Well, that's a good thing," the woman says. "It's always easier when the girl is the oldest. I'm sure she's a huge help to you. She's probably a second mommy to your boys."

At first, I am silent. Then I level with her. I just can't go on with this conversation anymore. "Look, I know you think you are asking harmless questions, but you should know that our oldest son just died, less than two months ago."

Her reaction of horror is immediate. It's as if I have thrown ice water on her. "How? Was he sick?"

"No," I say, absolutely incredulous that this conversation is continuing and causing me even more pain. "He was hit by a car."

"Oh my God. I'm so sorry. I'm so so sorry. I had no idea."

And suddenly I desperately need to get away. My goal was to celebrate with Baila, and perhaps enjoy the wedding, but now I feel like a walking tragedy. Without a word, I leave.

Later in the week, when I tell Karen about the wedding, she shakes her head. "That was an insensitive question," she says. "Asking about somebody's children is very personal. She had no right to put you in that situation."

But here's what I learn: People *always* ask how many children you have. It's an extremely common question, on the same level as talking about the weather, your job, and where you live. Yet now I understand that it's an incredibly loaded question for bereaved parents, and for couples struggling with infertility or miscarriage.

I wonder how many times I have unwittingly caused this pain for others. I know, now, to never ask. Instead, when I am introduced to new people, I wait to hear if they mention children—because inevitably, they will, if they have any. That's my cue, and the question I ask is, "How old are your children?"

From their answer, I can work out how many children they have now. That's how I avoid asking the question, but my own vigilance does not protect me; I am still asked the question. And every time I am asked, I hesitate, because there is really no good way to answer.

This predicament is discussed often in my Jewish bereaved parents email group. Everyone has a different approach. Some always include their dead children. Some prefer not to. At first, I am determined that my count will include Dovie. But I discover that when people realize that my oldest has passed away, the conversation changes entirely. They are asking what they believe to be a harmless question, and I am replying with a catastrophe. People can't handle it, so they respond by asking for more details, which I'm not always prepared to provide. What it boils down to is this: Do I want to share these private, painful details of my life with people whom I've just met? Because there is no way to mention Dovie without doing so.

It takes me a long time to realize that, in most cases, the easiest solution to my dilemma is to not include Dovie in my count. It greatly pains me to do this. The truth is that I *want* everyone to know I was his mother. I want to whip out pictures so they can see how beautiful he was. I want to talk about how he loved *Star Wars*, the New York Yankees, and *Harry Potter*. I want to tell them, allowing myself the tears in my eyes, how desperately I miss him, and how I would do anything just to be given the chance to hug him again.

But such raw emotions have no place in small talk. So I nod. I smile. I play the game, and I forever dread the inevitable question. And when asked, I ignore the stabbing pain in my heart, swallow my tears, and politely respond, "Four."

Chapter 37
Mikvah - September 4, 2006

It's been three months since we lost Dov, and Tzvi and I have decided that we are going to try to have a baby.

It has not been a simple decision to make. Since our trip to Virginia Beach, Tzvi and I have spoken at length about all the possible problems that may arise as a result. If I become pregnant quickly, I will be thirty-nine years old when I give birth. And because of my age, it might be harder for me to conceive. The pregnancy will probably be riskier, and the chances of complications will be much higher. And I know, perhaps better than many, that anything can happen; that there are no guarantees.

Yet still, I desperately want this baby. I feel like all our lives are now solely defined by loss, and I want to focus on creating something new.

Before we decided, I spoke with Karen, my grief therapist, about my doubts. "What will a new baby do to my family?" I asked. "Will it just be an added stress for all of us? We've already been through so much. I'm afraid that adding a baby to the mix will just make things more difficult."

"You'll definitely be busy," agreed Karen, "but I think it will be good for you. I've counseled families who had children after the death of a child, and they have all done well. I think it's a wonderful idea. And I also think that you're very lucky indeed that you have this option. Many parents don't."

I considered that for a minute. I thought of the many bereaved parents I'd met who were in that precise situation. It wouldn't be long before I myself might be too old to conceive. I realized that if this was the direction that we wanted to take, then we could not wait much longer.

I realize that getting pregnant and giving birth will require help from God. I am not at all sure that He will hear me; in fact, my experience has shown that there's a good chance He will not. But I do need to try. I leaf through prayer books, trying to find something appropriate that will help my request reach the heavens—but I find nothing. There are no prayers written specifically for a mother who has lost a child, and who now wants another one.

True, I could simply recite a psalm or two. Or I could just speak as I feel. But I realize that I have never in my life made an important speech without first knowing exactly what it was I was going to say. If I were going to voice a request to the President of the United States, I would certainly prepare beforehand. And if I believe that, when I am praying, I am addressing the king of kings, then certainly I should prepare as well. And so the day before I am scheduled to go to the mikvah, I sit down at my kitchen table and write a prayer of my own.

The night I am to immerse, I bathe as usual, inspect my nails, comb my hair, and set off for the Silver Spring mikvah across the street, clutching the prayer I have composed in my hand. As I enter the warm waters, I ask the attendant, a little sheepishly, if I might have a few minutes to myself to say a prayer before I immerse fully. She readily acquiesces and leaves the room.

Alone and naked in the waters of the mikvah, I unfold the slip of paper in my hand and begin to read.

Our Father, Father of mercy, I stand before you as I fulfill the mitzvah of tevila in the month of Elul, when You listen intently for prayer, and from the depths of my soul, I ask that You hear my plea.

It was Your will that my firstborn, Dov Matityahu ben Tzvi Hirsch, be taken from this world at an early age. I questioned Your judgment, but never did I deny that You were there. In the darkest hours of my life, I continued to believe in You. I believe in You still. I believe that You heard me those days that I prayed for Dovie in the hospital. I believe that You hear me now. Master of the Universe, during the most devastating time in my life, when You took my precious son from this world, I sanctified Your name.

And now I implore You to alleviate my suffering by granting me another child. Give me a healthy child, a child filled with goodness, a child filled with love, a child who will grow in the ways of Torah and live a long life. Grant me and my family comfort, so that we may find happiness in our lives once again. I beg You to heal our shattered home and our broken hearts. Look upon us with favor, and allow me to sanctify Your name again by showing the world that You have not forgotten us.

I beg of You, do not test me or my family again. Give us no more sadness, sickness, pain, or death. I implore You, do not abandon me in my time of sorrow. Heed my prayer as you answered Chana and so many others before me. Strengthen me so that I may continue to walk in Your path, so that I may be a good Jew, a good wife, a good mother, and a good daughter. Help me along this difficult road on which You have placed me.

Our Father, Father of mercy, I beg of You, please hearken to my prayer.

After the attendant returns, and I immerse myself, I wonder: Was my prayer heard? I cannot be sure.

Later, Tzvi and I sit upstairs in our bedroom, listening to classical music on the radio. It is our seventeenth anniversary, and he has bought a bottle of wine and a slice of brownie to celebrate. As we sip wine together, a battle of doubts begins to be waged inside my head.

Am I out of my mind? Am I really ready for another pregnancy? How will I handle the demands of another child? What will adding a baby do to our family? What guarantee do I have that the baby will be healthy?

How do I know that this baby won't someday cross the street and get hit by a car?

The doubts attack me until I begin to plunge into despair. I'm a fool, I realize, for thinking I can get pregnant and have another child. I'm an idiot for thinking that I can ever be happy again.

And then, from somewhere far away, I hear the voice of the radio announcer, telling us what piece we have just been listening to. And the words of the disc jockey announcing who was playing it catapult me back to a world of hope; the world where we make music with what's left.

"That was Itzhak Perlman," he says.

YANKEES GAME | 195

Chapter 38
Yankees Game

As the summer weeks pass, our friends continue to reach out to us. Every Shabbat afternoon, Judy visits, and we sit and talk. We also have two other regular weekly visitors: Dovie's friends, Ari Rosenberg and Mickey Cooper, who stop by every Shabbat afternoon to share their impressive collection of Star Wars toys with Noam and Avichai.

Rabbi Jeff Frances is another of our dear friends whose kindness during these hardest months we will always remember. Jeff teaches at MJBHA, in the middle school where Tzvi is the principal. He knew Dov well, or well enough to know that he was a huge fan of the New York Yankees. During his hospitalization, the Yankees were taking part in a four-game series against the Boston Red Sox. Among the many get-well emails and cards we received at that time, Jeff would fax us regular updates about the team that we could read to Dov as he lay unconscious. He also arranged for a box to be delivered to us filled with Yankees T-shirts, hats, and other paraphernalia, as well as tickets to see a Yankees vs. Orioles game in Baltimore in September. It was a gesture that had warmed our hearts and made us feel lucky to have such a good friend.

When the day of the game arrives, our kids are excited. We have never attended a baseball game before. They dress up in their new Yankees shirts and hats and we head to Baltimore, where—unsurprisingly, since it's a home game—we find ourselves greatly outnumbered by Orioles fans. No matter. We head for our seats, sip some juice boxes, and relax.

I am fine until I hear the baseball music start playing. That's when I realize that Dov never attended a Yankees game, and that he should have been here to enjoy it with us. *Why hadn't we ever taken him to a game? His entire room was decorated with Yankees flags and posters. For God's sake! Why hadn't we ever arranged a day like this when he was alive?*

I try to control my emotions, but at a certain point Tzvi sees my face, and I know he knows what I am thinking. I look into his eyes and collapse onto his shoulder, sobbing. I don't have to explain anything; he just holds me until I catch my breath.

This, I find, is the greatest regret of a bereaved parent. The realization that you have completely lost any and every remaining opportunity to be with your child; to celebrate birthdays, to ride bikes, to read books, to share meals, to attend a baseball game together. Even to do homework together. You thought there would be so many more instances of these moments to share, and now you realize that you should have savored every minute, because that time was so fleeting, and you cannot get it back.

When I lift my head, I see the kids watching me carefully. *I need to control myself,* I think. *This is just a stupid baseball game. Get a grip.*

I wipe my tears away and will myself to conquer my emotions. I want my kids to enjoy the day, and they can't do that if I am having a breakdown.

So, I bring myself under control. In my mind, I tell myself it is just a game, even though I know I am lying.

It is much more than just a baseball game. We are diving headfirst into Dovie's dream day, he isn't here to be a part of it, and he never will be.

Chapter 39
High Holidays

I have tried. I have truly tried to take Esther's words to heart, and to not blame myself. But as the high holidays approach, the time of year when we are judged, the time of year when our fates are sealed, I cannot help it. No matter what anyone says, I feel like there must have been something we did wrong. Something we could have fixed, and that if we had, Dovie would still be with us.

It was the mezuzahs. I'm sure of it. Or it was not giving enough *tzedakah*. One or the other.

Mezuzahs are supposed to guard our house and our family. They're supposed to be checked every couple of years, and the truth is that, before the accident, I can't remember when we had looked at them last. We should have had them inspected earlier. Why hadn't we?

It's not surprising that we were told to check them immediately after the accident; when something terrible happens, it's a common practice. Rabbi Malka *did* find them all to be kosher, despite some minor flaws. However, he said there were two areas in the house that qualified halachically as doorways and didn't have mezuzahs, so he put some up in those spots for us—and replaced the flawed, albeit kosher scrolls. When we came home from the hospital, we saw that he had placed the new scrolls in plastic bags and hurriedly affixed them to our doorways with gray duct tape. That's how they remained throughout the shiva;

no delicately carved wooden or crystal boxes with a Hebrew letter shin housing our mezuzahs, just Ziploc bags and duct tape—clear evidence of our desperate attempt to rapidly right what might have caused the wrong.

For months afterwards, I would see those duct tape mezuzahs and wonder. If we had had the forethought, the zeal, to check our mezuzahs earlier, might we have prevented Dov's accident?

Had I known then what my mother knew, my conviction about the mezuzahs would have only been strengthened. My mother had been with Rabbi Malka as he sat and unrolled each of our mezuzah scrolls, carefully inspecting each letter for cracks or defects which could have rendered the mezuzah unfit for use. He had beckoned her closer to show her a tiny hole that had formed in one of the scrolls. This in itself was not unusual, and did not necessarily affect the kashrut of the mezuzah, but the location of the hole was enough to make my mother gasp audibly; it had formed between the words *"u'v'lechtecha bad-erech"*—"and when you go out in the street."

Seeing my mother's reaction, the *sofer* had apparently realized that showing her the hole was not a wise idea. He tried to dismiss it, telling her it meant nothing; that people try to read meaning into such things, but they are meaningless. The mezuzah was kosher and that's what mattered.

But the damage had been done. My mother carried the weight of that experience for a long time, and finally broke down and told me the story, years later, sobbing at the memory.

But perhaps the mezuzahs had not been the problem. Perhaps we did not give nearly enough *tzedakah*. For months after the accident, I am certain of this. And I am sure that it was my fault. I was in charge of the family finances, and I often neglected to give as much as we should have because, well, to be honest, there was never enough to cover our basic expenses. Being observant, as everyone Jewish knows, is expensive. Kosher food, Shabbat, frequent religious holidays, synagogue membership, day school tuition, Jewish summer camp—it all adds up.

Of course, we gave regularly, but not always the ten percent of our earnings that was typically recommended.

Still, when Dov was in the hospital, we wrote checks every day, giving hundreds of dollars to worthy causes, even though we were not at all sure how we would pay for it all. We didn't care. All we knew was that giving *tzedakah* might make a difference for Dov, so we gave. Now I think that perhaps, if I had been more careful, if I had cut down on our expenses more and balanced our budget better, if I had given more regularly, Dov would be alive today.

No, actually, the more I think about it, the more I'm convinced that it wasn't a lack of *tzedakah*. It was probably that we didn't invite guests over often enough. I know some families who have guests over for Shabbat meals on a weekly basis. But after days of juggling work and the kids, I was often tired, too tired to cook a gourmet meal, entertain, and then spend hours cleaning everything up afterward. It was often easier to not invite anyone. I had been complacent, often not inviting guests for weeks on end. But maybe I should have. Maybe that would have made the difference.

What did I do or not do to cause Dov's death? Because I am sure, absolutely sure, no matter what anyone else tries to tell me, that it happened because of me. As Rosh Hashanah gets closer, these thoughts trouble me to the point of obsession. But rationality begins to creep in, and one day I realize that I cannot be the only person in the world who doesn't invite guests every week, doesn't check mezuzahs regularly, and doesn't always give a full ten percent to *tzedakah*. *If Dov died because of these things,* I think, *then there would be a lot more dead children.* No, I clearly must have done something worse.

I hear that a reputable kosher butcher in Monsey, New York has been discovered to have been cheating his customers for years. He has been buying non-kosher meat—which is much cheaper than kosher—repackaging it, selling it as kosher, and pocketing the difference. The idea horrifies me. Only once can I remember actually coming close to erring with keeping kosher; I was in college, busy running from one evening class to the next. I ate spaghetti and meatballs for dinner, and then, a half hour later, I unthinkingly purchased a pint of milk at a vending machine. I was halfway through the carton before I realized my transgression: We typically wait six hours after eating meat before having any milk. Some have the custom to only wait three, Scandinavian Jews only wait one, but a half hour? *A half hour?* I bolted to the bathroom, spat out the milk that was still in my mouth, and rinsed my mouth out with water over and over again. I even contemplated going into a stall and sticking my finger down my throat, but I realized the deed was done, I couldn't right it. So instead, I stood next to the bathroom sink and looked at my dismayed self squarely in the mirror. *This must never happen again,* I told myself. *I must never again consume anything without thinking about what I am putting in my mouth.*

I cannot imagine what it must have been like to discover that for years, you, your family, and your entire community have actually been consuming *treif* meat. I cannot imagine what it must have been like to have to replace pots, silverware, and crockery that were used unwittingly to cook and serve non-kosher meat. I wonder if the affected families felt the urge to vomit, like I did, when I realized what I had done. And in the back of my mind, I think about that butcher who had been selling forbidden meat to an entire community knowingly, for years, and I wonder: *Are all of his children alive?*

I cannot approach Rosh Hashanah feeling like this.

Last Rosh Hashanah I prayed, as I always did, asking God to forgive my sins, and to grant long and healthy lives to me and to my family. On Yom Kippur, I prayed and I fasted, as I had done for decades, beseeching God to seal all of us in the Book of Life. But clearly, my prayers didn't work. I messed up, somehow, and Dov is dead.

How do I approach God this year? How can I promise not to repeat my mistake, when I don't know what it was?

Tzvi knows how I'm feeling, and he also knows, from having tried, that he can't reason with me. Extreme grief has taught us both that feelings are not necessarily rational. This is why he tells me that he thinks I should talk to someone about my fears.

"I'm already seeing a grief counselor," I reply.

"That's not what I mean. You need to speak to a rabbi you trust. Share your concerns and see what he says."

I am dubious that anything will help, but I finally agree to make an appointment to see Rabbi Yitzchok Breitowitz, the rabbi of the neighboring community of Woodside, whom we know to be a learned and kind man. We have asked him questions about Jewish law before, but nothing quite like this.

On the morning of our meeting, I drive to the Woodside shul and sit with him. I don't need to explain what happened with Dov. He knows, as does the entire community. I open my mouth to speak, to tell him of my guilt, but instead my eyes fill with tears. I cannot even form the words on my lips.

He waits.

"I don't know how to get through Rosh Hashanah this year," I eventually say. "I keep thinking that what happened to my son was my fault."

"Your fault," he repeats. "And what exactly did you do?"

"That's just it. I don't know."

"I can't imagine that you did anything worse than most people. In fact, knowing your family, I would think that you approach mitzvot on an even higher level than the average person."

"But I must have done something. Everything happens for a reason."

"Mrs. Klugerman, we *do* believe God does everything for a reason, and that He does everything for the best. You are right; there is a reason that your son died. But we will never know what that reason is. It could be because of something completely unrelated to you. It could be because of something that happened generations ago. You will never know."

My tears are falling freely, and I try in vain to wipe them away. "Rosh Hashanah is coming," I say, with great difficulty, trying to enunciate the words without completely breaking down. "We say that *teshuva*, *tefilla*, and *tzedakah* remove the evil decree. If I had done those things correctly last year, wouldn't my son have been spared from this tragedy? Clearly, I did something wrong."

"We don't necessarily say that *teshuva*, *tefilla*, and *tzedakah* removes the evil decree," the rabbi corrected. "We say it *delays* the evil decree. The decree remains; the question is when it will take place. Or you can look at it another way: Some people say that *teshuva*, *tefilla*, and *tzedakah* remove the evil decree in the World to Come. So, conceivably, you did everything right last year, and your actions allowed your son to enter through the Gates of Heaven."

His words turn my understanding of Divine justice on its head. I wonder if any Jews have any idea what they are saying on Rosh Hashanah and Yom Kippur. I certainly didn't. It always seemed simple to me: You do good, you get good. If something bad happens, it's because you've done something wrong. And while I realize, of course, that it obviously cannot be that simple, and that plenty of good people have suffered in horrific ways, there's a part of me that needs to know, without a doubt, that Dov's death wasn't my fault.

I try again. "Some people think this could have happened because of *ayin hara*," I say. "Is that a possibility?"

"*Ayin hara* is a very serious thing. There are ways to determine if it's at play here. But I doubt this is because of *ayin hara*, and I would advise against pursuing that idea further."

"But if I don't know what caused it," I say, "how can I prevent it from happening again?"

The rabbi looks in my eyes. "Mrs. Klugerman, you must not dwell on why this has happened. In fact, I would even venture to say that feeling guilty about your son's death is your *yetzer hara*, your evil inclination, doing its work. Thinking like that serves absolutely no purpose, and it prevents you from moving forward. Instead, as difficult as it may be to accept, you need to repeat to yourself, over and over again, that everything Hashem does is for the best. Everything Hashem does is for the best."

The very idea that God has decided that Dov is better off dead makes me feel ill. I don't say so, but I am not at all sure that I can accept such a statement. Still, the rabbi's words help to alleviate my worries. I hold him in high regard. And he has assured me that, despite my misgivings and feelings of guilt, Dov's death was not my fault.

He is not the only rabbi I turn to for help before the High Holidays. It dawns on me that on Yom Kippur, for the first time in my life, I will be required to say Yizkor, the memorial service for the departed. Traditionally, this has been a time when I, like many other young people, have left the synagogue sanctuary, to allow people who have experienced loss to participate in the service without being observed by those who haven't. Typically, only people who have lost a very close relative recite Yizkor, and so I have never said it. Since my parents are still young and healthy, I hadn't expected to say it for many years. The notion of saying it now makes me feel queasy. I picture myself in shul, reciting Yizkor with Dov's name, and I see myself completely breaking down. I think I will not be able to bear it.

I broach the subject with Tzvi. "Isn't there some sort of leniency that allows new mourners to forgo Yizkor during the first year after a death?" I ask him hopefully.

"Nonsense," Tzvi replies.

"I don't know how I'm going to get through Yizkor," I tell him. "I don't think I can do it."

"Speak to someone you trust," he advises me again. This time, I get in touch with Rabbi Yaakov Bieler, the spiritual leader of Kemp Mill Synagogue, which is located about a mile from our house. We have known Rabbi Bieler since we first arrived in Kemp Mill, and I have always appreciated his scholarship and no-nonsense approach to halacha. I feel he can answer my question. I also am not sure what to do about my children; since they have lost a sibling, should they remain in shul for Yizkor as well?

I send him an email. This is what he replies:

Dear Yaffa,

I am of course sad that you find yourself in such a painful predicament. Life is full of challenging moments, but this, without a doubt, is one of the most difficult.

I am much more rational than metaphysical in orientation. Consequently, although the mystical literature does talk about how remembering those who are no longer with us is an *ilui* to their *neshamot*, Judaism has always seemed to me to be more about the living than the dead, and we have to do what is best for ourselves, in order to assure our continuing observance over the long haul. Just as, in the case of *pikuach nefesh*, we believe that it is better to violate one Shabbat in order to better be able to observe many, many Shabbatot in the future, I think that the same applies in this case as well. So whether or not you attend Yizkor this year should not be primarily informed by what its positive or negative effects will be upon Dovie's soul. The relevant question is what will the effect be upon your and your childrens' souls.

While I ordinarily tell people that the custom not to attend Yizkor during the first year following the death of a loved one is inappropriate, nevertheless there are people who follow such a practice. If you believe that participating in this *tefilla* would engender too much trauma for you and your children, I certainly defer to your judgment, and you could justify such an action by invoking this custom that is widely practiced. According to the rule that there is no such thing as a *minhag shtut*, it seems to me to be entirely appropriate to rely on this *minhag* in your case.

As for your younger children, I agree with you that they should not be in shul. Regarding the older ones, perhaps you can discuss this with whichever professional they may be seeing in the aftermath of the tragedy. Different individuals react differently; some are in need to confront the situation, while others require protection and a downplaying of the loss. Is it appropriate to leave the issue up to them individually?

I am not certain that your assumption that Yizkor will be easier to participate in next year is necessarily the case. It is true that the passage of time takes away some of the immediacy of the loss, but I imagine that this tragedy will continue to be devastating to recall and confront in the years to come. So you have to think clearly regarding when you want to begin confronting the situation, sooner or later. How will what you do this year affect what you will be ready to do next year?

At KMS we encourage everyone to stay in shul for Yizkor because we also say *mishebeirach*s for *Tzahal*, the *harugei Sho'ah* and victims of terror. Consequently, no one knows for whom someone else is saying Yizkor. Would it be helpful to focus upon someone else in your family, or even a friend or teacher who is no longer with us, rather than your son, and in this way "ease into" the situation?

I hope that my responses are appropriate and I have not been insensitive to you and your family's deep pain.
Sincerely,
Yaakov Bieler

I read the response several times before I realize that Rabbi Bieler has not given me a definitive answer, just some guidance as to how I might make my own decision about how to proceed.

It is true, I realize, that this is not just a decision for the present. How I act now could set the tone for how I will deal with this issue in the future. The pain may lessen at some point, but it will never really go away completely. It seems clear to me, therefore, that I will need to say Yizkor this Yom Kippur; avoiding it will not lessen the pain, it will only delay it.

As the holiday approaches, my anxiety grows. How will I get through these holidays? I will be asking God for forgiveness. Shouldn't He be begging me for mine?

Many in our community, to their credit, are sensitive to how we are feeling. A family sends us a Rosh Hashanah gift: a beautiful honey dish, along with wishes for a sweet year. Messages arrive by mail and email telling us that our friends are thinking of us.

And then, right before Yom Kippur, the most solemn day of the Jewish calendar, something unexpected happens.

I have been searching for them for years, and now, tempting me from an eBay listing, I find them: Four Ethan Allen Country French ladderback chairs. Each one costs a cool $409.99. Ridiculously expensive, in my opinion, considering that they must be at least twenty years old, even though they look like new.

When we bought our dining table, over a decade ago, we purchased six chairs to go with it. But then our family grew to outnumber the chairs. We would use folding chairs to supplement them, especially when company came to visit. I had looked to buy more chairs, but discovered that the style was discontinued. So I started checking eBay, month after month—but I had never found the elusive matching chairs until now.

I have no business looking at these chairs and, truthfully, I am not even sure why I went searching for them. I certainly have more important things to be doing. For the next twenty-five hours, I will not eat, drink, or wear leather shoes. I will stand in synagogue and pray to God for a long and healthy life for my family and for me, even though I know, better than anyone, that sometimes it seems like God just doesn't give a damn. Nevertheless, the chairs call out to me. I click on the different views and discover, to my astonishment, that not only is the wood stained perfectly to match the chairs we currently own, but even the plaid fabric upholstery on the seats matches. It's almost as if they were meant to be mine.

Still, I hesitate. The irony is just killing me. Until May, we had outnumbered our chairs. That wasn't the case anymore.

"The fast starts in an hour," calls Tzvi. "What are you looking at?"

"Nothing."

But he is already beside me, staring at the screen. "Ebay? Before Yom Kippur?"

"It's nothing." My index finger is already poised to click off the screen.

"You found our chairs?"

I sigh. "It's stupid."

"Just a minute." He sits beside me. "You've been looking for these chairs forever. Why not buy them?"

"Too expensive," I say. "And what is the point?"

"Get them," says Tzvi, pulling me back to the present tense. "Put it on a credit card. We could always use extra chairs."

I'm not so sure. We have four children now, and I have no plans to invite any guests—not now, not ever. I have no real expectation of celebrating or laughing ever again. My life as I knew it is over.

But my mother-in-law, who is visiting for the holiday and loves furniture, sides with Tzvi. "Buy them," she says with conviction, as soon as she sees the computer screen. "You'll see. You'll use them."

"It's so expensive," I protest.

She peers at the price. "I'll pay half," she says. "Just get them."

And that is how, on the eve of the most difficult Yom Kippur of my life, four dining room chairs purchased on eBay force me to acknowledge that there just might be a time in the future when we will once again fill our dining room. That there might eventually be a time when we will celebrate. A time, I think, when I might just be a little less unhappy than I am now.

On the night of Yom Kippur, Tzvi dreams of Dov for the very first and last time. Dov appears as a young boy with curly blond hair, and he is handing Tzvi an enormous shofar.

"Dovie," Tzvi says, "I can't blow this. It's too big. Bring me my shofar, the one I always use."

Dovie is silent, but his eyes are insistent. Once again, he tries to give Tzvi the shofar.

"Not this one, Dovie. This is much too big. I will not be able to blow it. You know the one I use. Bring it to me."

Dov silently tries once again to hand the gigantic shofar to Tzvi.

"No, Dovie. This is not the one. Bring me the regular one. You know which one it is."

Dov gently pushes the giant shofar to Tzvi, who realizes that he has no choice. The shofar is so large and heavy that Tzvi can barely lift it. Carefully and with great effort, Tzvi raises it to his lips, takes a deep breath, and blows a powerful, clear tekiah *that seems to shake the world.*

As the shofar is blown, Dovie watches and smiles.

The next day, I stand in synagogue, trembling, as I say Yizkor for the first time. I discover that, to my surprise, it's over in a few minutes and is not nearly as difficult as I thought it would be. Before I know it, people are filing back into the synagogue to continue with the service, and I am astonished, because the event I had been dreading for so long is already behind me.

Chapter 40
Sukkot - October 2006

Shorts, T-shirts, skirts, underwear. I pack our suitcases with care and tears. I shouldn't be crying, but once again, I can't help it.

This was supposed to be the family trip to Florida that we had been planning for years. We had intended to go to Adina and Avi for *yomtov*, then to Disney World and Universal Studios for *chol hamoed*. For months, we had saved up our frequent flyer miles, and we traded them in for airline tickets just before Dov died. And now, we will be going to Florida without Dov.

Rearranging the trip has not been simple. Our dear friend Fran Kritz spent hours on the phone with the airline, arranging to have Dov's ticket cancelled, our miles refunded, and our seats reassigned so that we would sit together. My mother-in-law, who always joins us for the holidays, will instead be going to my parents in Connecticut; my parents graciously invited her so that we can leave without worrying that she will be alone.

I should be excited, but a part of me is dreading the trip. At night, I lie in bed and weep, thinking about how thrilled Dovie would have been to go. We had taken the children to Florida only once before, six years prior, and had always hoped to return. Dov knew about this trip and had been looking forward to it. The thought of being in Disney World without him is devastating.

My emotions are even more volatile because I've just confirmed that I'm pregnant. It's so early that only Tzvi and I know at this point. I swing dizzyingly between feeling joy and hope one minute, and complete horror and fear the next.

When we arrive, Adina and Avi greet us with love, and they try their best to keep us smiling. We swim in their beautiful pool before the holiday begins, and snap pictures in which we are smiling and having fun. In their Sukkah, we joke about the hot weather, something completely foreign to us with our Maryland experience. We eat delicious food and attend synagogue. But walking by the perfectly manicured lawns of the palatial houses in Miami Beach only reminds me of just how shattered our lives are. *These people live perfect lives*, I think. *I have nothing in common with them.*

"I have something to tell you," I say to Adina when we have a quiet moment to ourselves. "Something big."

Adina looks at me. "Go ahead."

I take a deep breath. "Our kids don't know this yet, but I'm pregnant."

Adina's eyes open wide. "What? Wait a minute! Is this a good thing? Or a mistake?"

I start to laugh and cannot stop. "Of *course* it's a good thing," I finally say, between gasps. "What do you think?"

"Just making sure. Okay! So, this is great news! Oh my God! How are you feeling? When are you due?"

I tell her that it's so early in the pregnancy that I haven't even been to a doctor yet, but if my calculations are correct, I'm due to give birth sometime in June.

"I'm feeling fine physically," I say, "but at times I feel like an emotional wreck."

"That's understandable," she says. "But wow, this is *so* amazing. I am so excited!"

"But Adina, what if I'm doing the wrong thing? Is this going to make things worse?"

Adina considers for a minute. "You're not doing the wrong thing," she says. "You have great kids. This will be another great kid. This baby will only make your lives better."

Early in the morning of the first day of *chol hamoed*, we pack up enough food for four days and leave for Disney World. Adina takes her kids as well; they will stay at a hotel while our family will check into a condo. After over three hours of driving, we spend the day together touring around the Magic Kingdom with little Binyamin Simcha, and pose for a picture with the six living members of our immediate family—our new reality. Adina and I wear matching bandannas and recreate a photo with Pinocchio that we had taken in Disney World as children decades before. Only once do I feel close to tears: when the parade starts marching down Main Street, and I realize, once again, that Dov should be here to see this. I feel the sob rising in my throat, but I look at Avichai's delighted face and swallow my sadness. This is his first time in Disney World, I realize. I will not ruin it for him.

The next day, Adina stays with her kids in Disney World, but we decide to go to Universal Studio's Islands of Adventure theme park. Adina has advised me that, no matter what, we must go on the Spider Man ride. Tzvi, Noam, and Avichai refuse to join us, but Sarit and I stand in line for an hour, until she sees the ride and decides not to go on it after all.

Dejected, I return to Tzvi and the boys. We try a few more attractions with more success, until finally I confide in him. "Tzvi," I say, "I really want to go on that stupid Spider Man ride."

Tzvi is silent for a moment. "I'll take you," he says.

We leave the children outside the ride with Sarit, and wait in line. I am nervous, but determined to go. The two of us howl with delight as the ride twists, turns, and dives while following a holographic Spider Man. When it's over, I realize, with some surprise, that I'm smiling.

And that's when it hits me: it's the first time since Dov died that I have expressed a desire to do anything at all.

Chapter 41
Bereavement Retreat - October 20, 2006

Despite the wintery chill in the air, it's not hard to imagine warm and fun-filled summers at Camp Simcha in Glen Spey, New York. As Tzvi and I haul our luggage to our comfortable guest room, I wonder if that is exactly the point: the understanding that even though the immediate atmosphere is currently cold, one can look around and envision the promise of better times.

During the summer, children battling cancer and blood disorders convene at Camp Simcha for medically supervised overnight camp experiences. The camp is run and paid for by Chai Lifeline, an organization with a mission to help seriously ill Jewish children, their families, and communities. This Shabbat, Tzvi and I are among the thirty or so couples and families who have traveled here to attend Chai Lifeline's Healing Hearts Bereavement Program. It dawns on me that there are likely parents attending whose children, now deceased, once attended this camp.

Friends have told us that the event can be very therapeutic, but Tzvi is not convinced that it will help us. Prior to going, we argued back and forth; Tzvi didn't want to go, I insisted it was a good idea, and he finally relented. My parents are watching our children so that we can be here, and we drove all day Friday to arrive in time.

As we take our seats for Shabbat dinner, we discover immediately that small talk here takes on another meaning entirely. "What are your names?" we are asked. And then, "Did you lose a son or a daughter?" And then, "How did he die?"

Within minutes of meeting, the people at our table are sharing their horror stories. A daughter who lived for years with a childhood disease and one day simply didn't wake up. A son who was killed in a car accident. Some people lost their children recently, but for at least one couple we meet, it has already been a decade. Some, we discover, are here for their third or fourth time. We all hail from different places and different religious backgrounds, but we all share the shell-shocked look of people who have inexplicably and suddenly suffered great loss. The food is delicious and plentiful, and as we eat, we talk and talk and talk.

Undoubtedly, it's a relief to be speaking so openly with people who can immediately relate to what we have been experiencing these past few months. They understand the pain, guilt, anger, grief, regrets, questions, and the very real concerns about how we can possibly move forward. There's certainly a lot of baggage to unpack this Shabbat—meeting so many people carrying around so much pain is overwhelming.

After dinner, men and women break up into separate discussion groups. We don't separate for religious reasons; rather, we are told that women and men tend to discuss and react to their grief differently, so separation helps facilitate meaningful conversation. In the women's group, we sit in a circle and each woman introduces herself, states where she is from, and how and when she lost her child.

"I'm Yaffa Klugerman, from Silver Spring, Maryland," I say. "Five months ago, my fourteen-year-old son Dov crossed the street from his Yeshiva to our house, and was hit by an SUV."

I'm the only one in the group with a story like this. The vast majority, I discover, lost their children to illness, and most died when they were babies. I am clearly the one with the most recent loss. Yet as I look around, and listen, I get a sense of what may or may not be our future: Some women have gone on to have other children. Others have moved to new homes and new communities. But all are clearly still grappling with their losses, because all of them are still here.

When we return to our room that night, Tzvi and I talk about the conversations. He tells me how, when the group discussed faith, one father spoke about God having a grand plan and his belief that his child's death was ultimately for the best.

As usual, Tzvi was not one to mince words. "I took one look at him," Tzvi says, "and told him, 'You don't believe a word that you are saying.'"

"What did he say then?"

"He didn't answer, because it was true. You could see it in his eyes."

The next morning, we rise early to dress and daven. Throughout the day, we hear speakers, share stories, and eat copious amounts of food. In one session, a therapist speaks about different stages of grief, and then reads all the names of the attendees' deceased children as our eyes fill with tears.

Tzvi and the man whose faith he questioned spend a lot of time talking. Later, I speak with a woman who had four daughters and a son. One day, her son inexplicably never woke up; she and her family immediately moved to a different house and she later gave birth to another girl. *Did moving help?* I want to ask. But clearly it didn't, because she is still grieving.

"I keep hoping and praying that it will get better," she tells me. "But every day I wake up, and it's just as bad as before."

We share our stories. A father relates that he was once told that his son died because of his sins. A mother admits that she cannot stop feeling guilty about her daughter's death. We talk about burial customs, Kaddish, and epitaphs. We laugh and we cry, and I realize that, within just a few hours, we've made some very close friends.

But by the time Shabbat ends, we are emotionally drained. On Saturday night, we gather in the dining room and share photos of the children we have lost. Looking through them, I realize that every parent we've met has experienced an absolute catastrophe. It feels like we are all essentially characters in a Stephen King novel.

By Sunday morning, we hug our new friends and promise to stay in touch, but we are ready to leave.

"I was wrong," Tzvi says as we drive away. "This weekend was surprisingly beneficial."

"Really? How so?"

"I learned that I never want to become a parent who still attends bereavement retreats years after my child has died."

I think of the family whose son died a decade ago. Ten years from now, will I still be feeling the way I am feeling now? I hope not.

"I agree," I say.

I had heard that Chai Lifeline only allows families to attend the bereavement retreat up to four times. I'm not sure if the thinking behind this is for practical reasons or for emotional ones. After all, Chai Lifeline cannot possibly accommodate all bereaved families every year. But maybe there's also some gentle prodding built into the policy which suggests that perhaps, after four times, it's time to move beyond bereavement retreats.

On the way home, we decide to stop at the grounds of Camp Morasha, where we have spent countless summers, with Tzvi working as the boys' head lifeguard and me coordinating the camp newspaper. This past summer was the first time in ten years that we had not gone. Friends from Morasha told us that after Dov's death the camp decided to redecorate the shul on the boys' campus and dedicate it in Dov's memory.

As we travel familiar roads that we have not seen in a year and a half, the memories begin to rise. They are at every turn in the road; by the time we arrive at camp, I can feel hundreds of them, swirling along the path to camp along with the autumn leaves that have fallen from the trees.

We park the car and begin to walk. Here is the lake, where Tzvi spent the majority of his time for ten summers. I remember taking the kids for dips on Friday afternoons, and Tzvi and I stealing time to swim together. I look towards the center of the lake and remember us canoeing together, and our children learning to swim.

Here is our cabin, with seven hooks still hung outside to store our raincoats. Here is the porch, where we gathered to enjoy pre-Shabbat snacks after going out for ice cream. Here is the desk where I worked on the camp newspaper. Here is our bed, where I sat curled up with Dov and Sarit one Friday evening, each of us absorbed in our own copies of the newest *Harry Potter*. Here is the bathroom, where we showered the kids and wrung out their muddy bathing suits. Here are the bunkbeds where our kids slept and giggled together, the floor where they stored their books and games.

We follow the path up to the boys' shul, along which I have lugged countless baskets of laundry on my way to the camp's washing machines, and pass the boys' head counselor's office, where we would go to receive our mail. We pass the basketball courts, where Sarit went rollerblading, and Avichai learned to walk. We see London House, where we stayed during the summers when Noam and Avichai were infants.

We enter the boys' shul, where Tzvi davened regularly with Dov and Hillel. The camp has installed a new wood floor and decorated the walls with scenes from Creation. The *aron* is also new, and behind it is painted a ladder, reaching towards the heavens.

Then we see the plaque: "*L'zecher nishmat Dov Matityahu ben Harav Tzvi Hirsch Klugerman.*" We stand underneath, taking in the beauty of the surroundings, and the meaning of the words on the plaque. Then, as my tears begin to fall, I sit down on one of the newly painted bright blue benches. Tzvi sits beside me and we hold each other, weeping quietly.

There are no campers' shouts in Morasha that day, no announcements on the loudspeaker, no golf carts whizzing down the hill. All we can hear is the rustle of the leaves, the whispers of our happy memories, and the sound of our sobs.

Chapter 42
The Pregnancy - December 2006

"Stay at the table, please. We are having a family meeting."

It's a typical weekday night, and our family has just finished eating dinner. It's somewhat unusual, however, that Tzvi is joining us. As a principal, he must often work late to attend meetings, but tonight he is present and is the one who calls our family meeting to order.

"Why are we having a family meeting?" Sarit asks.

She and Hillel, Noam, and Avichai look at us. I know what they are thinking: *Could it possibly be more bad news?*

"Are you going to tell them?" I ask Tzvi.

"Technically, it's your news to tell," he replies.

"No way!" says Sarit, who has guessed what we are about to announce. Then she turns to me. "If you don't tell them," she says, "then I will!"

I smile. "We are going to have a baby."

"Oh my God!" Sarit is bursting with excitement. "I can't believe it!"

Hillel has an enormous smile on his face. "A baby? When?" he asks.

"The official due date is June third," Tzvi says.

Avichai, as the youngest, is clearly trying to wrap his head around the announcement. I reach out to give him a hug. "You are going to be a big brother, Avichai!" I tell him.

Noam, who rarely gets worked up about anything, is processing this new information carefully. But I can see that he is excited.

"Can we tell our friends?" he asks.

"I am planning to tell my staff at our meeting tomorrow," Tzvi explains. "They have to hear this news from me. But you can tell your friends at midday tomorrow."

"*What*? How am I going to wait until then?" Sarit asks. She is jumping up and down. "I'm so excited!"

When she comes home from school the next evening, Sarit tells me how she watched the clock all morning. She and her class were rehearsing for a play, but at the stroke of noon, she suddenly left the stage.

"Where are you going, Sarit?" her teacher called. "We are in the middle of practice!"

"I have to take care of something! I'll be right back."

Sarit dashed out of the room to find two of her closest friends. "My mother is pregnant!" she yelled, jumping up and down. "We are having a baby!"

The news spreads quickly, and quite suddenly, I become much more approachable. Gone are the days when people only spoke to me in guarded tones, unsure if they were saying the right thing. Now I have somehow become a beacon of hope and renewal, and everyone is falling over themselves to offer congratulations and find out how I'm feeling. I didn't expect to suddenly become so popular—although I guess it makes sense. Anyone who knows us understands what this pregnancy represents.

When I visit a new obstetrician, she carefully looks over my medical history.

"So, you have five children?" she asks.

"My oldest was killed in a car accident in June," I reply. "So now I have four."

She looks at my growing abdomen, then at my face, and then she drops her face in her hands and begins to cry.

220 | THE BROKEN VASE

"Can I give you a hug?" she asks. Even though I am completely taken aback by this unexpected burst of emotion, I extend my arms. We embrace each other in the examination room—two women who have never met before. This is the effect I now have on people.

All of the people we tell—my parents, mother-in-law, siblings, friends, colleagues, and yes, even complete strangers—are overjoyed to hear the news.

"Every time I think of you," Adina tells me when we talk on the phone, "I start humming 'Circle of Life.'"

I'd like to say that I am feeling hopeful and joyous, as I'm sure many believe me to be. I certainly do feel some of that. But behind the smiles, thank yous, and hugs, I am still wrestling with grief, doubts, and despair.

Chapter 43
Dark Humor

There's something about intense grief that makes you appreciate humor in a slightly twisted way. Perhaps it's because we are so deeply surrounded by pain that certain occurrences strike us as funny. Perhaps it's the body's way of releasing some of the intense pressure.

Among the hundreds of condolence cards we receive, for example, is one from an old friend who apparently didn't get all the facts straight. Throughout the card, she expresses her deep sympathies for the loss of Hillel, and continues to do so for several paragraphs. At first, I am taken aback, but then I just start to laugh. I think of her trying so hard to find the right words to say, and then screwing it up so thoroughly. It sounds a bit cruel, but I will always remember that card and the much-needed laugh it gave me.

That's not the only time when the morbid strikes me as funny. When Tzvi's birthday approaches, in December, I take the kids to CVS to pick out a card. After several minutes of looking around, Hillel runs over to me while clutching a card excitedly.

"Ema, I found the card for Daddy!"

The outside of the card says, "Dad, thanks so much for always sticking with us through all our misfortunes, calamities, and disasters." And then, on the inside, it says, "But enough about my brother..."

"You see?" says Hillel. "It's *perfect*."

"Good God," I say. I am horrified. "We can't get this for Daddy."

"But why not?"

"Because...because it's awful. Oh my God." And then I start to laugh, because the whole situation is just so ridiculous. I stand there holding what is arguably the most inappropriate birthday greeting card for my husband ever, and I can't stop laughing. (But I still don't buy the card.)

And then there's the time when I am at Judy's house, and another woman is there with her son, who gives her a huge hug. I am not sure why, but just seeing this boy embrace his mother reminds me that I can no longer hug Dov. It upsets me so much that I abruptly leave and come home, where I sit in the kitchen and cry.

"What's wrong, Ema?" asks Noam, who has come into the kitchen for a snack.

"Well," I say, "I saw something that reminded me of Dovie, and so it made me feel sad."

"Oh," says Noam, trying hard to sympathize. "Did you see someone get hit by a car?"

"Um, no," I reply, and then I start laughing. He's asking me such an outlandish question with such genuine concern, and for a minute, it makes me forget my pain. I hug him instead, and we laugh together.

Chapter 44
Guilt - January 2007

On an icy Shabbat afternoon, Tzvi and I walk Avichai to a friend and then begin our return home. By now, it's apparent that I'm a few months pregnant; I have to stretch my coat to button it around my protruding belly. I walk slower than usual, a hint of the waddle that is so typical of expectant mothers.

We turn onto a street very characteristic of Kemp Mill: The houses are well kept, the yards are landscaped, and the traffic is almost non-existent. In pockets between parked cars, snow piles high, close to the curb. As I walk, I hear the crunch of snow and ice beneath my feet. It is so very unlike Arcola Avenue here. The air is so still and quiet that I am certain that someone standing at the end of the block would be able to hear the echo of our footsteps. "I love these houses," I tell Tzvi.

He turns to me. "Please tell me you're not thinking of selling our house. Are you?"

But that is exactly what I am thinking. Herein lies the answer to my prayers: A quiet street, with very little chance that any more of our children will be killed by speeding vehicles.

"Because," he continues, "I know that the kids want to stay where they are."

I stop in my tracks and look at Tzvi, and all at once, without warning, I cover my face and begin to weep.

"I'm such an idiot!" I cry. "It's my fault! It's my fault!"

"Yaffa—"

"If we had only lived on a street like this, Dovie would be alive! I *knew* there was something wrong with the house when we bought it! God, I *knew* it! But like an idiot, I went ahead and bought it! And now he's dead!"

Tzvi puts his arms around my shoulders and I cry into his chest, my sobs echoing up and down the quiet, still street, which I am sure is filled with happy families who have never dealt with a tragedy like ours.

"He would still be alive," I finally say, wiping tears from my face, "if only we lived someplace else."

Tzvi lifts my chin so I face him. "Yaffa, Dov would still be dead. Don't you get it? Hashem decided that our son was destined to die. Where we lived had nothing to do with it. In fact, living in that house was a great kindness that God gave us."

"*What?*" I practically spit the word. "What *possible* kindness was it to live in that house?"

"Because," says Tzvi, his voice shaking, "when Dov was hurt, *you were there*. In his last moments of consciousness, you were by his side, talking to him. That happened because we lived there."

I cannot stop crying, but his words reach my pained soul, and slowly, they begin to resonate.

"Yaffa, listen to me. Either we believe God is involved with our lives or we don't. Do you understand? *There is no in-between.*"

THE ROBBERY | 225

Chapter 45
The Robbery

I arrive home from work and am stunned to discover that the window next to our front door is broken. *How bizarre,* I think. *Maybe it was a deer?* The deer had increased dramatically in the area, and I had, on occasion, seen them in my backyard, even though we lived on a busy street. It wasn't impossible that perhaps a deer had run into the window and broken it.

This is my twisted thinking. In my mind, it is more plausible to think that a random deer has broken our window, than a burglar. I enter our house and immediately notice that the back sliding door is open as well. *Well, that's weird.* But this sight just confirms my initial assumption. *I must have left it open by mistake, and a deer came in and then broke the front window.*

But what are the chances that a deer would voluntarily walk into a house and then into a window?

Slowly, the reality of the situation forces its way into my head. *It wasn't a deer. Someone broke into our house.*

I leave the house abruptly and call the police from my car. "I think someone broke into our house," I say. "And they still might be there."

Two officers arrive within minutes and walk into the house. By the time they finish looking around, confirming that a) we've been robbed, and b) the robbers are gone, the kids have come home from school and are waiting with me outside.

One police officer holds an empty piggy bank.

"That's mine," says Noam. "It was full."

With the help of the police, we look through the house and discover that not much is missing. My silver candlesticks are still on display in the dining room, and our laptops sit on the table there as well. My jewelry has not been touched. The only thing missing is a wad of cash that Tzvi kept in the bedroom for emergencies, and the money in Noam's piggy bank.

"My guess," says one officer, "is that they broke the window, reached in and unlocked the door, headed right for the bedroom, found the cash, and left as quickly as they could out the back door."

"Can you dust for fingerprints?" I ask.

"We'll do that. But I have to tell you, we probably won't find them."

I am stunned. There are hundreds of people who walk on our street every day. Ours is one of the few busy streets in quiet Kemp Mill with constant traffic and pedestrians. We always felt that the position of our house provided more security; we presumed burglars would be less likely to break into a house in such public view.

I check with my neighbors and ask at the Yeshiva across the street. I find out that there is a camera on our road, but its range doesn't reach far enough to show what happened at our house. Nobody has seen or heard anything, and the idea that someone got away with breaking our front window in broad daylight shocks everyone.

Tzvi tells me he had close to a thousand dollars in his night table. It was money he had earned doing freelance work, and he tells me that he was saving up to buy me a piece of jewelry. And Noam's piggy bank had been completely full, after years of saving coins.

After the police file their report and leave, I sweep up the broken glass and dust, and call someone to fix the window. It will be replaced with one that is harder to break, and our lock will be replaced as well.

A part of me is not surprised. I already feel like God has turned His back on us, and the robbery just reinforces my thinking. It's just more proof that we are completely vulnerable and unprotected. Anyone can break into our house and get away with it. I try to console myself: At least the thief didn't take the silver, or the jewelry, or the china. Money can be replaced, I reason, even though it might take time to do so. At least we weren't home when he broke in. We—or rather, what remains of we—are safe.

What I don't expect is how the robbery traumatizes my kids. After losing a brother, I figured this was a minor incident, but that doesn't turn out to be the case. They talk about the robbery for months. Long after it is behind us, the kids continue to check that we have locked the door and ask if there is any chance that someone could break in while we are sleeping. On top of the trauma of Dovie's death, they now fear for their safety.

I know what they need to hear. I hug them and reassure them that we are safe, even though I know, better than anyone, that even with the greatest precautions, anything can happen.

Chapter 46
The Trial - February 2007

I play back the message I have just received from Detective Murphy, who investigated Dov's accident, letting us know that the driver who hit Dov will appear in traffic court tomorrow, contesting her speeding ticket and the $110 fine that goes with it.

I am incredulous and call the detective back immediately. "What exactly *is* this?" I ask when he picks up his phone.

"I'm as surprised as you are, ma'am. I just looked at the docket and saw that she is scheduled to appear tomorrow, so I thought you'd like to know."

"What does this mean?"

Murphy pauses. "It means she is saying that the investigation drew the wrong conclusions, and that she wasn't speeding. She's saying that she's not at fault."

"Can she *do* that?"

"She can say what she wants. The evidence was clear that speed was a definite factor. But I do suggest that you and your husband come to court tomorrow. The judge may want to ask you a few questions, but even if not, it's still important for you to be there so the case won't be thrown out."

I am shaking my head. Once again, I cannot believe this is happening. "So we have to sit through the descriptions of the accident and how it occurred?"

"I'm afraid so, ma'am. I will be there to testify so that the facts are clear."

"And let me get this straight: She's doing this to avoid a fine of a hundred and ten dollars? *That's it?*"

"And points on her license, no doubt. But I imagine she wants to assert her innocence most of all."

I am, quite frankly, incredulous. And horrified. "What time does it start?"

I hear the detective rustling some papers. "Be there at eight-thirty in the morning."

My thoughts flash back to my summers working as a teacher at Camp Morasha in Lake Como, Pennsylvania. One of my favorite lessons began with me writing a word on the blackboard, slowly and deliberately: MURDER

The word attracted the attention of the many sixth-grade boys who had not yet found their seats. The boys were eager to play sports, go swimming, and do pretty much anything other than sit in a daily *shiur* on a beautiful summer day. The classroom was airless, the ceiling fans did little to cool us off, and empty soda cans littered the floor, even though food and drink were prohibited in the classrooms. Holding the attention of a class full of boys under these circumstances was never easy, but I had my tricks. Sometimes I grabbed their interest by telling them a good story. Other times I began with a game. But for this particular lesson, the only action I needed to take to hush the campers was to simply write this word on the blackboard.

The boys found their seats and stared at the word.

"Is that what you want to do to us?" one boy finally asked, breaking the silence, while others giggled.

I didn't respond. Instead, I faced the blackboard again and wrote:

INVOLUNTARY MANSLAUGHTER

"What's the difference?" I asked them, and then I put a finger to my lips and raised my hand, because someone would inevitably call out the answer.

"I know!" said one boy, waving his hand excitedly. "Call on me, Morah Yaffa!"

"Yes, David?"

"Involuntary manslaughter is by accident. Murder is on purpose."

"How, exactly, can you kill someone by accident?"

Another kid interjected. "That's easy. You—"

"Hands, please!"

Several hands waved in the air. "Moshe?"

"You can be cleaning a gun and then the gun can go off by accident."

"Good example," I said. "And now, here's one more phrase." I turned to the blackboard and wrote:

CRIMINALLY NEGLIGENT HOMICIDE

"Anybody have any idea what this means?"

One boy gingerly raised his hand.

"Yes?"

"It's death by accident, but it's because someone wasn't careful enough."

"Excellent," I said. "And as it turns out, we are reviewing all of these terms because this week's *parsha* talks a great deal about criminally negligent homicide and how the Torah responds to it."

I turned back to the blackboard and wrote in Hebrew:

IR MIKLAT

"What is this?" I asked.

David waved his hand wildly. "It's a city of refuge. That's where people went who killed someone by accident."

"Good. And why did people go there?"

Mark raised his hand. "They go there because otherwise the family of the person who was killed will want to kill the murderer. So people go into the cities of refuge to protect themselves."

"Perfect," I said. "Now, Rambam actually spends a lot of time talking about the cities of refuge and who goes to them. He divides criminally negligent homicide into three types of cases."

I wrote on the blackboard: *Shgaga krova le'oness.*

"The first case is what Rambam referred to as accidental, but close to uncontrollable," I explained. "So, let's say, boys, that

I am driving down the road near camp, where the speed limit is fifteen miles per hour. I am abiding by the speed limit. And then suddenly, a boy falls from a tree onto my car, and he is killed by the impact. Would you say that was an accidental death?"

The boys nodded. I had their complete attention.

"Rambam discussed cases like this, where the death was not preventable, and where it was unrelated to negligence. If such a case would have occurred during the time of the *arei miklat*, the cities of refuge, the Jewish court would probably have determined that I was blameless. That's because boys usually don't fall from trees onto cars. And in such a case, I would not have to go to the city of refuge."

I wrote a new term on the blackboard: *Shgaga*, which means "accidental."

"But now listen to this case: Imagine for a moment that I am driving down that same road, only this time I am driving at twenty-five instead of fifteen miles per hour. And then a child unexpectedly darts into the middle of the road, and I hit that child, and she dies. What then?"

"That's a different story," Moshe replied.

"How so?"

"Because you weren't careful enough."

"Ah," I said. "But it was an accident. I didn't mean to kill that child."

"It's still partially your fault."

"Very good. This, boys, may have very likely been a case that, in the time of the cities of refuge, would have qualified me for the *ir miklat*. According to Rambam, a person sent to an *ir miklat* is slightly negligent, and that's what we have here. After all, I wasn't speeding excessively. But, as Moshe said, I should have been more careful, particularly so close to a camp where young children could be playing."

I wrote one more term on the board: *Shgaga krova leZadon*. Loosely translated, it means, "accidental, close to on purpose."

"And now, boys, imagine that I am driving down the same road, only this time I am driving sixty miles per hour, and I am driving drunk. A child walks into the street, and I hit the child and kill him. What then?"

"You're toast," said David.

"But it was by accident," I protested.

"It was almost on purpose," said another boy.

"Good," I said, "because that's exactly how Rambam referred to it. When a person is so grossly negligent that someone else dies as a result of their negligence, that case falls outside the realm of the cities of refuge."

"Wait," said one boy. "Wouldn't you still go to the *ir miklat*?"

"I would not," I said. "They would not allow me in, because I was far too negligent."

"But then what happens?"

I taught this lesson many times, and I knew to pause for the maximum effect.

"What happens," I said slowly, so that they hung on my every word, "is that the family of the murdered child *has every right to kill me for my negligence.* And so, I am doomed to spend the rest of my days looking over my shoulder and fearing for my life."

I taught this lesson every summer, and it was always fascinating to see the boys get involved in the discussion. I would review a list of real-life murder cases taken from newspaper articles, and I would ask the class, reviewing each case: Would this person enter the *ir miklat*?

And now, in a tragic twist of irony, my son has been killed in the very situation that I had used in my class debate, and the driver is about to appear in court. Would she have been sent to a city of refuge? I try to think rationally. Clearly, it was an accident, and it was not brought about by the kind of reckless negligence where she would be rejected by the *ir miklat*. But the level of her culpability is debatable. Dov wasn't in a crosswalk, but then again, so many pedestrians cross in that very spot all the time. As a resident of the area, she should have known to be careful. Many motorists drive at speeds higher than the thirty mile per hour limit, but just because others do it doesn't make it right. There are several schools on Arcola Avenue; what business did she have exceeding the limit when children were in the area? It's clear, I think, that this is a classic *ir miklat* case. The driver who hit Dov would surely have been sent to a city of refuge.

In biblical times, families had the right to avenge the death of a member murdered accidentally if there was some negligence involved. If we were living in those times, the driver who hit and killed Dov would have had to flee to a city of refuge, or else I could have legally killed her. Would I have done so?

There may be no cities of refuge anymore, but I believe that the feelings of the departed's family are very much the same. I cannot imagine actually killing anyone, but the anguish of losing Dov is so horrible that I understand why others would want to.

Tzvi and I meet Detective Murphy and the county lawyer as we enter the traffic court building the next morning. We shake hands, and the lawyer—a blonde woman named Maddie—tells us that they appreciate us coming. We take our seats in the courtroom and listen to one traffic case after another. I have never been in traffic court before, but it doesn't take long for me to realize that no matter how serious the infraction, the judge is likely to reduce the fine and points if the defendant simply shows up.

I scan the courtroom, searching for the driver, but I can't find her. Truthfully, I can't remember what she looks like. The only time I ever saw her was when she was weeping on Arcola Avenue after the accident, and I was too focused on Dov at the time to recall anything about her except that she was female.

So, I do what I often like doing when I have nothing to do: I take out a notebook and pen and I write. I write about the expressions on the faces of the defendants called up to explain their parking violations, many who have clearly been here before and know the routine well. I write about the nearly dozen violations that are dismissed simply because the police officer neglected to show up. I write about the judge who presides over it all, with an "I've seen it all" expression that suggests she wants nothing more than to get through her docket and make it home in time for the six o'clock news. I write about it all, and I wait for our turn.

But when the judge finally calls up the driver, who pleads "not guilty" to her $110 speeding ticket, it is immediately clear that our case is different than the rest. Unlike the rest of defendants who have come today, the driver has a lawyer to help plead her case. There are witnesses present. Detective Murphy is there with counsel as well. The judge takes it all in and quickly concludes that our case is not one that will be decided in the typical five to ten minutes that it has taken to decide the rest. She proposes that we move to a nearby courtroom, and calls in another judge to preside over the remaining cases left on the docket.

In the new courtroom, I scrutinize the driver's face, which is as unfamiliar to me as any stranger's would be. She is African American, trim, and looks to be in her late forties. I could have been alone in an elevator with her and I still would not have recognized her. She stares straight ahead, not showing any awareness that she is being watched.

Then it begins. The attorney reviews the all-too-familiar facts of the case: That at four fifteen p.m. on May 31, 2006, Dov Klugerman crossed Arcola Avenue without being in a crosswalk. That the driver—who had no prior record of wrongdoing—was in an SUV in the middle lane that hit him.

The driver contends that she was not speeding and could not have avoided the accident.

The counsel calls up a lone witness, who had been driving the vehicle directly behind the driver and saw the accident. He swears Dov leaped in front of her at the last second, and she could not have stopped in time.

Maddie reviews the case as well: She calls up Detective Murphy, who testifies that an investigation concluded that the vehicle was traveling at a speed of not less than 42 miles per hour in a 30 mile per hour zone. He notes that the car's impact was so hard that it propelled Dov a distance of seventy feet, he landed on his head, and eventually died from his injuries. Then he displays a detailed chart indicating where the vehicle was and where Dov was when the accident occurred. He shows where they recovered his hat and shoe at the point of impact, and where Dov's body lay, so far from the SUV that hit him.

I am shaking again. *Be calm,* I tell myself. *Think of the baby.*

Tzvi and I can do nothing but sit silently and watch. At one point, I feel the judge looking at me. I return her gaze, and hope that my eyes will communicate what I desperately want to say: *Don't go easy on her,* I think. *She screwed up. She didn't mean to, but she did, and as a result, my beautiful son is dead. Don't forget that my son is dead.*

And then the defense calls up the driver, who slowly makes her way to the stand, not even giving us a glance. She says she has lived in the area for years and has had no prior vehicular accidents.

"Tell us about the day of the accident," says her attorney. "How fast were you going that day?"

"Maybe twenty-five at the most," she responds.

I want to scream, *nobody does 25 on Arcola Avenue!*

"How do you know you were doing twenty-five? Did you check your speedometer?"

"No, but I live around here. I know the area. I never speed."

If you don't check your speedometer while driving on Arcola, I think, *then you are speeding.*

"At what point did you see the young man who crossed the street?"

"I saw him as I was approaching in my car. He stood off to the side, waiting at the curb. He saw me coming. Our eyes met. He hesitated. And then he darted across the street."

"Did you try to stop?"

"I tried. I truly did. But I couldn't stop in time." Her voice breaks with emotion. "I've been traumatized by this incident since it happened. But I know that there was no way it could have been avoided. I slammed on the brakes. I tried to stop in time. But it was impossible."

"Your Honor," concludes the attorney, "we believe the sentence is unusually harsh."

She has to pay $110 and has some points on her license! I nearly shout. *I have to bury my child!!*

"A similar case with a speeding violation would not result in such a steep fine as well as points on the license," he continues. And I know it's true, because that's precisely what we've been witnessing all morning: Points thrown out, fines reduced, cases dismissed, just because the defendant bothered to show up and deny wrongdoing.

But it's not going to happen here. I stare at the judge, daring her to look in my direction and dismiss the charges. If she shows mercy to the defendant, she will have to do it in front of the parents who are now bereft of their son.

The judge indeed glances our way. "Detective Murphy," she says, "did the speed of the vehicle contribute to the outcome of the accident?"

Murphy rises. "Definitely," he says. "At a lower speed, the young man would likely be alive today."

She purses her lips. "I can reduce the fine a bit," she says, almost apologetically, to the attorney, "but I'm afraid, under the circumstances, the points will have to stand."

It is a small triumph. Although I am still incensed that the fine is being reduced, I am absolutely certain that the judge would have ruled differently if Tzvi and I hadn't been here.

As we file out of the courtroom, I follow behind the driver. Tzvi grabs my arm. "Wait," he whispers. "Stand back. Wait until she leaves."

But I have plenty to say to her. There are no cities of refuge to which she can be banished, but at the very least, I want to grab her and force her to look me in the eye. *Tell me you're sorry!* I want to scream. *Tell me you made a mistake! Tell me you're overcome with guilt! Beg for my forgiveness! But for God's sake, don't you dare tell me you had nothing to do with it!*

But Tzvi holds me back and, together, we watch her leave.

Chapter 47
Pesach

Years ago, my mother advised me to keep a Pesach journal to record memories of the holiday. I followed her advice; every year, I would write about the challenges of cleaning and cooking, the guests we invited, the places we visited, and my hopes and wishes for the new year. But as the once-joyous holiday approaches, I wonder how I will write this year's entry. How will I write that, this year, we spent Pesach without Dov? How will I write of the pain that fills our hearts? That our lives have been forever shattered?

The problems and challenges I used to write about seem so petty. This year, Pesach is an immense hurdle that I fear will destroy me. We have to find some way not just to get through it, but to celebrate it, despite the anguish in our hearts. We are faced with an enormous challenge: how do we rejoice when we are weeping inside?

It's a problem we have been confronting all year. On Chanukah, our children unexpectedly received an enormous box of toys and games, courtesy of Chai Lifeline, which brought smiles to everyone's faces. That same week, Yitzie and Ruthie invited us to their house in Passaic, New Jersey, for Shabbat. It was lovely to be with them for the holiday, but I blinked back tears when I saw how my nephew Dani—exactly one year younger than Dov, and closer with him than any other cousin—often stood alone.

I found myself on the verge of weeping again before Purim, when our entire family gathered, as we did every year, for our annual hamantash making. After many years of preparing these triangular Purim treats together, we were like a well-oiled machine, and each person was assigned a different role: mixer, roller, cutter, filler, or pincher. The jobs rotated from one person to another so that everyone was given a chance to do everything. We usually made about two hundred hamantashen together, but this year was harder, because a beloved helper was no longer with us. *Oh, how Dovie had loved this!* I thought. *How is it possible that he will never do this again?*

As Pesach approaches, Tzvi and I decide that we will deal with our grief by keeping ourselves as busy as possible, and so we invite my mother-in-law and three of my brothers and their families for the last days of Pesach. All together, we will be twenty-one people, and the Prices next door, who are away for the holiday, graciously offer to house fourteen. We spend hours cooking and cleaning, and that allows us precious little time to think of our emotions, which is precisely what we know we need.

That's not to say we don't feel Dovie's absence as we work. The grief appears at random times, often out of nowhere: I am peeling carrots for chicken soup, Dov's favorite, and I start to cry. Or my eyes fill with tears looking over Dov's school projects, wondering how it was possible that these flimsy Pesach projects actually outlived him.

It does not help that our air conditioning and heating breaks the week before the holiday, and so I am getting estimates for new and expensive systems while also shopping for massive amounts of food. And it does not help that I am seven months pregnant, carrying what seems to be a very active baby, and dealing with the exhaustion and hormonal fluctuations that come with the territory. I feel tired and emotional all the time, and at one point, when I find out how expensive our repairs will be, I sit down, crying, and tell Tzvi that I think I am losing my mind.

"You're pregnant, the air conditioning and heating need to be replaced, Pesach is next week, and our oldest son is dead," he says. "I think that, under the circumstances, you're doing very well."

But despite everything, the holiday is not all grief. And we find that, time and again, as irrational as it seems, it is possible to laugh even when we are feeling the pain. The first Seder, which I expected to be excruciatingly painful, is actually beautiful, and we finish in record time: by 12:30 am! Maybe it helped that I wasn't drinking wine, or that the baby kicking inside me kept on reminding me to pay attention and focus on life. Avichai recites the *"Mah Nishtanah"* beautifully, Hillel and Sarit ask exceptional questions, Noam takes great pains to read accurately and clearly, and my mother-in-law raves about the food. The second Seder is harder, but somehow we get through it, and without crying. That, in itself, is a significant accomplishment.

It's strange, but I realize that despite the tragedy of losing Dov, we still feel fortunate. We have remarkable children, a loving family, an extraordinary community, a roof over our heads, and the means to celebrate the holiday. We have another child on the way, and Hillel's bar mitzvah next year. These are all good things. We know that we can't ever again speak as if we know what the future will bring, because we've learned that terrible, horrific things can happen when you least expect it. But we move forward, and we hope for the best. It's an extraordinarily difficult task, but what else can we do?

The awful pain is still with us, and we know it will never completely go away. Dealing with it is a constant struggle, and Tzvi and I finish the holiday both physically and emotionally exhausted. But the fact that we made it through gives me hope. If we did it this time, then surely we'll be able to do it again.

Chapter 48
Dovie's Room

It can't be avoided anymore. We have to clean out Dovie's room.

A part of me wants to leave it exactly as it is. Dovie's walls are still covered with his NY Yankees posters. His closet and dresser are still filled with his clothes. His books, trophies, baseball cards, and souvenirs are scattered around his desk. It's been months since we lost him, and I still don't even like to walk into his room, but it's got to be done. There is a baby coming, and we need the space.

I've been thinking for a long time about how to manage this. We have four bedrooms. Sarit has her own room, which faces the backyard; Tzvi and I are in the master bedroom; Dov had a small room that faced the front of the house; and Hillel, Noam, and Avichai share the large room at the end of the hall. The new baby, we have found out, will be a boy, so he will not be sharing Sarit's room. I think about asking Sarit to move to Dov's room so that we can use her larger room for two boys. But then I think better of it. She loves her room and has often commented on how she enjoys being woken by the sun that faces her window in the morning. She would hate a window that faces the Arcola Avenue traffic and the Yeshiva across the street. Forget it. I'm not asking her to move.

The easiest solution would be to keep everyone where they are and to give the baby Dovie's room. But I hesitate. Hillel is now the oldest boy, and he should be given the opportunity first. "Would you like to move into Dovie's room?" I ask him one day.

"I want Dovie's room to stay the way it is," he replies.

"I know how you feel," I say gently, "but we need to move Dovie's things. A new baby will be joining our family soon and we need the room."

Hillel considers this. More than any of our children, he has taken Dovie's death particularly hard. I worry about him all the time.

"Sweetie," I say, "you don't have to move in there. I just wanted to give you the choice. Someone will need to move into the room. If you don't want to do it, then the new baby will be there. It's up to you."

"What will happen to all of Dovie's things?"

"I will save everything in a big box. We can go through it anytime we want to remember him."

Hillel thinks it over and decides that perhaps he would like his own room. Now, all that is left to do is to go through the room. I dread it, but it must be done.

I buy a large plastic box at Target and tackle the task in one evening. It's not easy. I start with his closet, thinking I will just give away all of his clothing. But then I see how many items are new, bought specifically to conform to the dress code at his new school, and then the tears start to flow. I wipe them away. I need to be practical. *I have three more boys, soon to be four. Someone will wear these eventually. I'm not giving these perfectly good clothes away.* So I pack them up in a cardboard box and haul it down to the basement.

Then, before I do anything else, I get my camera and snap pictures of Dovie's walls. The posters will need to come down, but I need to remember how this all looked. And then I take them down, and pack them in the plastic box, along with his notebooks, toys, trinkets, and assorted junk. It probably would have been easier to pack it all up quickly, but I feel compelled to inspect everything carefully.

A part of me is both hoping and dreading I will find some sort of clue as to why Dov died. What would happen if I found drugs? It would indicate a troubled life, but it could also explain why the accident happened. Yet I find evidence of nothing except what we already knew: he was a teenage boy, with likes and dislikes. I find nothing out of the ordinary, but that makes it all the more heartbreaking for me.

Sarit is right across the hall, and she looks in to see me wiping my tears. But she also cannot deal with the thought of dismantling Dovie's room. She closes her bedroom door.

It takes several hours to sort through everything. I throw out what I believe to be garbage, and keep any shred of what might be valuable to us in the future. Someday, I think, I will need to explain to the unborn child inside me who his brother was. I will take out this box and show him. See the ceramic D he painted at a birthday party? And look at the journal he kept when he was in second grade.

This is what remains of my eldest son.

As I sort, and read, and pack things away, I cry softly, trying hard not to disturb the children. And in my womb, my unborn child, perhaps sensing that something is amiss, kicks and kicks and kicks.

Chapter 49
The Unveiling

Months ago, Tzvi and I had to decide what should be written on Dovie's tombstone. For a long time, we tried, but made absolutely no progress. We would sit at the dining room table together and start to discuss it, and within minutes, we were both sobbing. But we needed to have a headstone in place in time for the yahrtzeit. My mother suggested that we get in touch with my uncle, Aaron Boxer, who had written epitaphs in the past, and that's what we did.

Uncle Aaron visited a cemetery in Lakewood, New Jersey, where he copied down some epitaphs that had been written for children. He sent them to us. Then he wrote a poem using some of what he had seen. Concurrently, we asked our dear friend, Rami Isser, who writes well in Hebrew, to help us compose something in Hebrew. Tzvi and I sat with all the documents and took bits and pieces from each, and then added our own touches.

We learned that there are a lot of guidelines for the proper way to write an epitaph. Some rabbis say that including English dates are not appropriate, although we consulted with others who said they were fine. We also learned about burial expenses, which is probably why many epitaphs say very little, because every letter costs money.

When we finally agreed on the text, we ordered the stone, and then began to make preparations for the unveiling. We could choose a day for the unveiling that worked for as many people as possible, and so we decided to hold it on Sunday, May 13. My niece would be having her bat mitzvah in Baltimore the day before, and this would enable relatives who were in the area for the bat mitzvah to also attend the unveiling.

We make sure it is announced in our shul, so that community members can attend if they wish. And on Sunday morning, we head to Mt. Lebanon Cemetery, some fifteen minutes from our house. It will be our first time at the cemetery since Dovie's burial.

When we arrive, we find that a small crowd has assembled, about forty people, including relatives and many of Dovie's friends. Tzvi stands next to the covered tombstone to speak:

> Dov was our eldest; he was the first grandson for both the Weiss and Klugerman families. He was a brother, a cousin, a friend, but first and foremost, he was Dov.
>
> Dov loved his NY Yankees and riding his bike. He loved his mother's chicken soup. To this day, on Friday night, I remind myself of his penchant for a cup of chicken soup late at night after everything had been put away. Oh, and his unabated desire for potato kugel. Yaffa and I still remark on how much potato kugel is left over nowadays after Shabbat, now that Dov is gone. It's funny how the little things mean so much.
>
> Dov had the typical relationship with his siblings, alternating loving them and hoping they would stay away from him in public. But his love for them was evident to anyone who saw their interactions. I remember one time the kids were playing outside, and Noam was young, and he started to run after a ball that had rolled into the street. Dov and Sarit both leaped into action to hold him tight. When he got his own computer, Dov told me that in order to be fair I had to be ready to give each kid their own computer. I told him that Sarit would

get one; he told me that he knew Sarit would get one, but he worried that Hillel would feel left out.

Dov's loss deprives us all of so much. *Chazal* understood that the loss of a child does not only impact the immediate and extended family; the loss affects the community as well. In the third chapter of *Mishna Ta'anit* we read of a public fast declared because two children died tragically.

We have all lost a promising young man who loved Torah and empathized with other people. I remember Dov asking me about having kids over to our house for Shabbat who might not have a place to stay otherwise. And that was in anticipation of the arrangements needing to be made. Dov so much felt what others were feeling. During the shiva there were a few stories about Dov noticing young children who had been knocked down and going over and making sure that they were all right. From his bar mitzvah gifts Dov decided to give *ma'aser kesafim*, the tenth we give from our earnings, to an orphanage, because he could not imagine growing up without parents.

For quite a few summers, Dov would take a vacation from camp and visit his grandmother and keep her company. It was the good life for a few days. But as much as he benefited from the undivided doting of his grandmother, my mother benefited from the time Dov spent with her, and those days he was a regular presence at *shacharit* in the shul where I grew up.

Dov took *tefilla* very seriously. When the students at the Academy finish eighth grade, there are awards given, and the teachers recommend students for different awards. Rarely are there unanimous nominations. Dov was unanimously nominated for the boys' *tefilla* award.

Yes, we have lost a wonderful boy and for each of us, the loss is acutely painful. But for me, I have also lost my *talmid muvhak*, my consummate devoted student. More than study with me, Dov studied me. He watched my every move; studying my *minhagim* and *hanhagot* and asking about my *piskei halacha* and how I allowed or why I decided against certain ideas and actions.

How do we come to grips with this loss?

Is there no balm in Gilead for our family and community? How do we understand this?

Yaffa, in her *hesped* at the *levaya*, repeated a thought from Dov's bar mitzvah *parsha*: the idea of a *chok*, a law, that seems to defy our comprehension. In yesterday's reading, we read of the *tochacha*, the rebuke, of what will happen if we are disgusted with God's precepts. The portion of *Bechukotai* begins with the seemingly strange formula of "If you will walk with my statutes."

Yaffa remarked to me that that is what we do with *chukim*, we walk with them, especially because we do not understand them.

Rabbi Tarfon in *Pirkei Avot* teaches: The day is short and the work is much to accomplish.

He continues: If you learn a lot of Torah you will get a large reward, and the taskmaster is trusted to pay you your true deserved wage.

But almost reading our minds, he concludes his *mishna* with: The reward for the righteous is in the world to come.

Their pure lives are theological challenges for us, because we do not see them receive their reward in this world.

I want to conclude with the following thought. As I mentioned, Dov was my *talmid muvhak*, my devoted student. Dov knew that I take fast days very seriously, and pushed himself to take all fast days as seriously as I do. I want to quote from the beginning of the *haftarah* read at *Mincha* on public fast days. It is taken from

Isaiah chapter fifty-five. The *haftarah* begins:

"Seek out God where He is found, call unto Him when He is close."

But continues: "My thoughts are not your thoughts and My ways are not your ways, says God. For as the heavens rise high above the land, so My ways rise high above yours, and My thoughts high above your thoughts."

We cannot comprehend God's ways. But as the incomprehensible ways of God are our *chukim*, we can only say that we will walk with them and continue to move forward.

We uncover the tombstone and Tzvi reads it aloud.
"Buried here is the light of our eyes and the first born of our hearts
Dov Matityahu ben Tzvi Hirsch Klugerman
Tamuz 7 5751 – 12 Sivan 5766
He poured out his heart before his creator with warm prayers
He loved the Torah with a great love
His heart rejoiced on holidays and Shabbat
And he always cared for the good of the other
And when he was returning home from Yeshiva
He didn't succeed in crossing the street
And was snatched suddenly from our hands
And rose to the Yeshiva on high
May his soul be bound in the bond of eternal life."

I watch the children. Avichai has just turned five, and it's hard for him to sit still. He walks around the graves, creating his own path, and I don't have the heart to stop him.

Everyone places rocks on the new tombstone, and then we are done. Our families follow us back home and keep us company. We put out some bagels and juice. It's been an emotionally exhausting day, and it feels good to be surrounded by loved ones.

Chapter 50
The Torah Dedication

For months, Tzvi has been planning the Sefer Torah dedication in memory of Dov. Originally, it was to take place on Dov's yahrtzeit, but we rethought that when we realized I would be due to give birth around then. We decided to move it up to Yom Yerushalayim, a great day to celebrate, which would fall out on May 16, 2007, during my ninth month of pregnancy.

As the date nears, the amount of preparation for the event is overwhelming. Tzvi wants the entire school to be involved in the ceremony, and the logistics are unwieldy. If all goes as planned, we expect a thousand people to attend, including the entire school—seven hundred students.

Tzvi and the *sofer* devise a schedule that should work. The ceremony will begin in the auditorium, with the writing of the final letters of the Sefer Torah. The honor will go to my father; MJBHA's head of school, Dr. Josh Levisohn; Young Israel Shomrai Emunah's assistant rabbi and Dov's teacher, Rabbi Rosenbaum; and Tzvi. After a dvar Torah and prayers, the audience will escort the Torah out to the school parking lot, to the accompaniment of a band, where there will be dancing in honor of the new Torah and Yom Yerushalayim. Finally, the Torah will be escorted to its new home, in the middle school *Beit Midrash,* where students in sixth through eighth grade gather twice daily to pray.

But before we get to the final ceremony, we wish to give many people the opportunity to write letters of the Torah scroll. Of course, few people are truly qualified to write letters in a Torah, but they are able to do so because the *sofer* outlines the letters, which the people fill in with ink, thus "writing" a letter. We create lists of people we wish to honor, and we begin by including the names of family members. While traditionally only men can write a Sefer Torah, the *sofer* assures us that there is a way to involve women as well. The one requirement is that everyone must be over bar or bat mitzvah age—twelve for girls and thirteen for boys.

On the Saturday night following my niece Meira's bat mitzvah, which is also the night before the unveiling and just three days before the Sefer Torah dedication, our family gathers at the *sofer*'s house in Baltimore. Among those who are there are me and Tzvi with our children, my brother Ari, his wife Deena, and Meira; my brother Akiva and his wife Nataly; my brother Yoni and my sister Adina; my brother Yitzie and his wife Ruthie, and two of their children, Miriam and Dani.

Only a few of the men actually fill in the letters on their own. In most cases, the *sofer* writes and the people assist: He grasps the quill and the person "writing" the letter very lightly holds on to the edge of the feather at the same time. We take turns: With the *sofer*'s help, I fill in a letter, although Tzvi does not, since he will be writing at the ceremony itself. After Sarit adds her letter, Hillel asks for a turn as well. We explain to Hillel that he is not yet old enough, as he has not reached the age of thirteen. But when Hillel's eyes fill with tears, I just can't bear it.

"Our son will be a bar mitzvah in January," I quickly explain to the *sofer*. "Can we possibly make an exception this one time?"

The *sofer* looks at Hillel wiping his tears, and beckons to him with a smile. We take a picture of them both: Hillel, the not-yet bar mitzvah boy, concentrating as he holds the tip of a quill gripped by the *sofer*, writing a letter in the Sefer Torah.

Later that week, Tzvi creates a list of all the male teachers in the school, as well as many dear friends. They will write their letters during the ceremony at the school.

"What about the women?" I ask. "We need to involve the women too."

The *sofer* agrees to have the women meet him in his bookstore, where he will help them write letters in the same way he did with our family. I make a long list of the many, many women who went to great lengths to help us this year: Judy Rosenthal, Barbara Price, Fran Kritz, Barbara Robbins. And so many, many more.

By the time we are done, we have close to a hundred names. Together, they will all help create this Sefer Torah, which will be used for generations. And suddenly I realize that this event is not just a way of remembering Dovie. It's a powerful way to help heal our families, friends, and our entire community.

On the evening before the dedication, I go to the bookstore and greet the dozens of women as they arrive. The *sofer* has set up a table and two chairs, and each woman gets a turn to sit with him and hold the edge of the quill as he nears the completion of the Torah. I watch them and realize that I am witnessing a truly extraordinary scene. *How often*, I think, *do women gather together to help write letters in a Torah?*

Barbara Robbins emails us soon afterwards:

Dear Tzvi and Yaffa,

I just wanted to take this opportunity to thank you both so very much for allowing me to be part of history. It truly was an experience that I will treasure and never forget.

I felt, as I held the quill, a connection to Dov, who took his learning of Torah so seriously. What a fitting tribute to such a fine young man, who displayed such kindness and unselfishness to all he came in contact

252 | THE BROKEN VASE

with. I feel very honored to have been a part of this and
I thank you both with all my heart.
With much love,
Barbara

The day of the Torah dedication arrives. Tzvi and I are
extremely nervous. No event of this magnitude has ever been
attempted at the school. The media has been invited to attend.
Our families—even those who were just here for Meira's bat
mitzvah a few days ago—are arriving from out of town so they
can take part. Dov's class and teachers at the Yeshiva of Greater
Washington will also be there. We have assigned responsibilities
as best as we can: Four of Dov's closest friends will hold the
poles of the chuppah that escorts the Torah. Teachers, students,
and family will take turns holding other *sifrei* Torah to join in
the dancing.

A video camera and screen have been set up so that the
audience can see the parchment as the Torah is completed.
Tzvi, as the master of ceremonies, explains each step and calls
up the last people to the Torah. I sit in the audience along with
hundreds of others, watching as my father, Dr. Levisohn, and
Rabbi Rosenbaum write their letters. The youngest children
in the audience have been chattering softly while this is going
on, but now, a hush descends upon us all as Tzvi approaches
the Torah. He closes his eyes and concentrates, and then takes
the quill and completes the final letters.

When the entire audience exits the auditorium to go outside to dance, I am amazed by what I am seeing: Hundreds of
students and teachers are dancing with *sifrei* Torah and Israeli
flags. Even the preschoolers are involved; they have created
hats with pictures of *sifrei* Torah that they have worn for the
occasion. I watch as our newly completed Sefer Torah is passed
from Tzvi, to my father, to my brothers, to Rabbi Rosenbaum,
to Jeff Frances; to so many people who carried us through this

year in the same way that they now carry the Torah—with care and love. Fran pushes my mother-in-law in her wheelchair to the middle of the girls' circle. Cindi, who has driven in from New Jersey to join us, is dancing as well. Everyone there has witnessed our heartache, and now, everyone is rejoicing with us as we dedicate this Torah in memory of Dov.

The students form two long lines, holding hands, creating a path of honor for the Sefer Torah. Those holding it dance down, within the two lines, making their way back into the school and to the *Beit Midrash*. I watch, remembering the cemetery, when the community formed two lines for us to pass down while they said "*hamakom yinachem*." I realize I am experiencing the complete opposite of that day.

We reach the *Beit Midrash* and, with great fanfare, the Torah is placed in the *aron*. Tzvi hoists Avichai to his shoulders so he can see. The singing finally stops, and Tzvi, in tears, recites Kaddish, while everyone around him answers.

Afterwards, the students break for lunch, and the adults meet in the cafeteria for a reception. I am speaking, and have thought long and hard about what to say:

> Good afternoon, and thank you for joining us today.
>
> Our son Dov, *alav hashalom*, had a very unique way of looking at things. One day he approached me – he must have been maybe eight or nine, and asked me, "How many letters are in the word shorter?" I counted the letters and responded that there were seven. Then he said, "how many letters are in the word longer?" "Six," I replied. He was silent for a moment. "So actually," he said, "shorter is longer than longer."
>
> That phrase, "shorter is longer than longer," became a very famous Dovie-ism that we repeated often. Sometimes, when he would be running out the door, I would call, "Have a good day, Dovie, and don't forget: shorter is longer than longer!"

In retrospect, I've looked at that phrase as something much deeper: it was a comment about seeing outside the box, about looking beyond what you would expect. Sometimes, we don't see the whole picture. Sometimes, shorter is longer than longer.

Those of us who knew Dov remember a young man who possessed a very strong love of Torah and Judaism. He took great pride in fulfilling mitzvot, and he loved to learn. I think he would have been fascinated with this Sefer Torah, and that he would have been very proud to be associated with its history and its legacy.

Dov's time in this world was far too short, but the dedication of this Sefer Torah will ensure that his memory and his love of Torah will continue, and will be imparted to others for many, many years to come. The Torah is compared to an *etz chaim*—a tree of life—so even though Dov is no longer with us physically, I feel in my heart that a part of him will live on through this Sefer Torah. It is a fitting tribute to the type of young man that he was, and all that he hoped to achieve.

This Torah was *pasul*, unfit for use. It happens to many old Torahs—their letters are cracked, their panels are frayed, worn, or ripped. At first glance, they sometimes seem to be beyond repair. How does one restore such a damaged Torah? Sometimes you cannot, and then the Torah must be buried. But sometimes it can be restored. It's a terribly long, arduous, painstaking process, which involves the checking of over three hundred thousand letters, many which must be rewritten. It seems like an impossible task—but it can be done. The Torah can be fixed. And it helps greatly when people wish to help.

A little less than a year ago, I think our family had much in common with this Torah. We were frayed, worn, and our hearts felt as if they had been ripped apart. We wondered how we could ever go on after losing Dov. How does one go on living after such a catastrophic loss?

But we learned that it is possible to go on. It's a terribly long, arduous, painful process. There are times when it seems like an impossible task. But it can be done. We know we will never be the same, and that the pain will always be there. But we found that we could still laugh, and we could still love. We could still lead meaningful lives. And what helped us most was knowing that people cared.

Much like the many who helped write this Sefer Torah, each person who reached out to us was in some way helping us go on with our lives. Every person who said "*hamakom yinachem*," every person who called to see how we were managing, every person who cooked, coordinated carpools, and did a million other things to help us, every person was helping to add new letters to the very worn and frayed pages of our lives. Every person who wished us strength was echoing the words of the Torah, which tells us "*chazak chazak v'nitchazek*."

And so I am here to thank you, not just for helping to dedicate this beautiful and meaningful Torah, but also to thank you for helping us live through this very difficult year. We have experienced an enormous and terrible loss, and we continue to grapple with it, but Tzvi and I see ourselves as very fortunate in many ways. We feel fortunate to have family, to have friends, to be part of this community, and part of the Jewish people.

I want to extend a special thanks to the Melvin J. Berman Hebrew Academy for working so hard to make this project a reality. We are incredibly grateful for everything they have done.

I want to thank all of you for joining us here, and especially the many people who took off work and traveled long distances to be here. We're honored and very moved that you could join us.

And finally, I want to thank the many, many people from across the world who participated in this project, from those who spent hours working out logistics, to those who bought *pesukim*, to those who filled in letters. Every gesture meant so much to us. We hope that this Sefer Torah will not only serve to honor Dov's memory, but will also give much-deserved honor to our family, friends, and community.

We thank you so much for participating.

The Sefer Torah dedicated in memory of Dovie is regularly used by the MJBHA middle school until this day.

Chapter 51
Yahrtzeit

Dov's first yahrtzeit is fast approaching, as is the due date of our sixth child, and my anxiety builds. Each time I think about the yahrtzeit, a small stab of fear strikes my heart. I know it will be a very emotional and difficult day—and a very public one, because it seems that everyone is aware of it. In the past few weeks, I have experienced the unveiling of Dov's *matzeva* and the *hachnasat Sefer Torah*, and I am completely emotionally drained. How will I get through it? How long will it take me to emerge on the other side? A small part of me is hoping that I will go into labor on the day of the yahrtzeit, because doing so will, in some way, allow me to skip the inevitable grief—and, I fear, despair—and proceed straight to better times. The thought of getting through the yahrtzeit is so daunting. What better than a birth to escape it?

On another level, there's a part of me that is hoping for a "happy ending." I desperately want a sign from God that it's time to move forward. Timing is everything; having a baby on Dovie's yahrtzeit, I believe, would be the ultimate message to us and to everyone who knows us that we have been granted an opportunity for a new beginning.

But it doesn't happen. On May 29, the morning of the yahrtzeit, I wake up as pregnant as ever. I sit in the living room and sulk. I didn't want to deal with this day. Why haven't I given birth yet? I feel as if I am carrying a load of bricks on my back in addition to the baby in my womb. The weight is so very heavy. I have been dreading this day, and so hoped to have a good excuse to escape it.

But there's a part of me that is not at all surprised: I have been forced to face so many, many, difficult events this past year. I wanted to move away from my house rather than constantly face the traffic in front of it, but I'm still here. I wanted to avoid holidays and happy events, always painful reminders of our loss, but I couldn't. On many days, I wanted nothing more than to curl up in bed, throw the covers over my head, and never get up again.

I faced each challenge. I got through each one, and discovered that I would be able to get through them again. Dovie's yahrtzeit is just one more difficult event that I have to face, if, for nothing else, to prove to myself that I can live through it, and do it again.

Throughout the day, family and friends call to express condolences, share memories, and see how we are doing. It is another long and difficult day, but we never feel alone. By the end of the day, I am relieved to be putting it behind me.

That night, I go into labor. I am euphoric. As the pains get stronger, I call Judy to watch the kids, and I pack my bag and leave for the hospital with Tzvi. I am admitted, and I practice my breathing as the moments tick by. But after an exhausting night, in the morning I'm still only three centimeters dilated, and the contractions slowly fade.

"We can break your waters, or even strip your membranes," says the doctor. "You're at term and you could deliver today."

But I have spent the entire night in labor and I am so, so tired. All I want is some sleep, and the last thing I want is to deal with more pain. So I grab my bag and Tzvi and I go back home.

Soon there's another significant date to face: May 31, the day of the accident itself, when Dov was hit by the SUV. That was the beginning of the end, when Dov was truly broken, and we did not yet know that he, ultimately, could not be fixed. There is no candle to light on May 31, and no rituals to perform, but I must do one thing.

Thursday, May 31, is a clear, warm day, much like it was a year earlier. At 4:10 pm, I exit my front door and walk to the curb. As usual, vehicles are passing in both directions. Across the street, Yeshiva students are attending class. I hear geese squawking at the Kemp Mill Park and see mothers pushing strollers. It is a perfectly normal day, just as it was a year ago.

When 4:16 arrives, I brace myself. I am waiting for something to happen. Any second, I think, there will be a crash, or an earthquake, or a nuclear bomb. Some sort of disaster undoubtedly will take place. I glance to my right and left, but nothing happens. Life goes on. There's something particularly unsettling about that. I see an incredibly uneventful and ordinary day, but in the back of my mind, I know that can change at any second. I realize then that I will always see the world this way. I will always be *hoping* for stability and a promising future, but I will always carry with me the knowledge that nothing is ever guaranteed. We live ordinary lives, and often forget how vulnerable we are; our worlds can be shattered in a second.

The next day, Friday, I go into labor in earnest. I feel the first hints of it when I am at work: little twinges of pain that I feel every so often. I check my watch. They are coming about twelve minutes apart. When I get home, I cook for Shabbat as usual while timing the contractions. It's not time to go to the hospital yet, but it will happen soon. After the table is set, after I have lit candles, and after Tzvi and the boys have come home from shul, we sit down to the meal and I find that I can't eat a thing.

"Ema, why aren't you eating?" Sarit asks me. Her friend, Aviva Rhein, is joining us for Shabbat, and the two of them are enjoying each other's company.

"I'm pretty sure I'm in labor."

Aviva's eyes look as if they will pop out of her face.

"When do you think you'll have the baby?" asks Sarit.

"Soon," I say, as I feel another contraction beginning.

By 11 pm, all the kids except for Sarit and Aviva have gone to sleep, and I feel like it's time to go to the hospital. Tzvi runs across the street to wake Judy and ask her to come stay. I tell Sarit and Aviva that we are leaving. Since it's Shabbat, we will not be in touch by phone until Saturday night.

Judy hugs me. "Whatever happens," she says, knowing the story of Noam's birth in our living room, "don't leave that hospital until you've had that baby!"

When we arrive at the hospital, I am sure that labor is progressing. The contractions are stronger and arrive more frequently. But when the nurse checks me, I am devastated to learn that I'm still at three centimeters—exactly where I was when I left the hospital a few days before. How is it possible that all of this laboring has accomplished nothing?

The nurse calls my doctor, who, knowing about my false labor a few days ago, opts to wait until the labor progresses further before heading for the hospital. She asks to be updated and then, I presume, goes back to sleep.

The nurse suggests that we walk around. As I do, the contractions become much stronger. I practice my breathing to get through each one. After nearly an hour, the pressure is intense, and with each contraction, I get down on all fours, forcing myself to breathe through each one. I can't endure the pain much longer. How long will it take to become fully dilated, if I started at only three centimeters?

"Order me an epidural," I gasp. "I can't continue like this."

Tzvi speaks to the nurse. It will take about twenty minutes until the anesthesiologist arrives. Until then, I keep on walking, and breathing, and panting, and dropping down on all fours to keep my mind above the pain. *This baby better be coming soon,* I think.

An hour after the nurse sent us to walk around, we return to her so I can be checked. She beckons to me to lie down on the table, but on the way, I am hit with an exceptionally intense contraction. I stop and grip the wall, throw back my head, and gasp for air as the pain completely envelops me. As it finally starts to subside, I feel the unmistakable sensation of something moving down, spreading my hips wide apart.

I lie down on the table as the pressure hits me again. This time, I roll to the side and try to keep breathing as my muscles shake and shiver. In the middle of this, my waters break.

The nurse checks me, but is speechless.

"How far along?" I demand to know.

"You're at ten," she says. "How can that be? I checked you just an hour ago."

Another contraction erupts. I know from experience that once my waters have broken, there's no way to breathe through the pain. It puts me in another realm completely, where I am barely conscious of the activity going on around me. But still I see Tzvi, standing right next to me.

"Yaffa, listen to me," he says, looking right into my face. "You are doing great. Do you hear me? You are doing just great!"

Then he turns to the nurse.

"She will give birth in ten minutes. You might want to call a doctor."

The nurse is so stunned by my progress that she doesn't move at first.

"You now have nine minutes. Would you like some help?" Tzvi asks. "I've done this before."

His words snap her into action, and she runs to the intercom. "I need help stat! My patient is giving birth now. Who's the resident on call? *Get him*!"

In minutes, the room is filled with people, and suddenly there's a great deal of activity taking place all around me, but I am unaware of anything except for the incredible pressure pushing this baby out of my body. It's as if there's a giant hand squeezing my insides.

"Can I push?" I wail. "I want to push!"

"Go ahead and push!"

In minutes, I feel the familiar stretching and burning below, and I know the baby's head is emerging.

"You're almost there!" the resident doctor tells me. "Don't push, just breathe."

And then the head is out and, with one last contraction, our new son begins his life with a healthy, robust cry.

Alive, alive, alive!

We are such vulnerable and exquisite creatures. How many systems in our body need to be aligned for life to be created and sustained? How many miracles take place with each breath that we take?

"Yaffa, he's beautiful," Tzvi says. "He's perfect."

The pain has stopped, and I look around me feeling as if I'm waking up to a new world. The nurse is canceling the order for the epidural. I say hello to the resident who just delivered the baby. I'm told that my doctor is on her way. And then I start to cry as I get my first look at this extraordinary child, who has joined our family in spite of our great pain.

Sometimes, it is our task to find out how much music we can make with what we have left.

"We are so glad you are here," I tell my son, as my tears fall. "Welcome to our family. We are so glad you are here!"

THE LIGHT | 263

Chapter 52
The Light

Tzvi and I have already decided on the name of our son. He will be called Meir, which means, "to bring light." After the darkness of the past year, we are ready for happier times, which we hope he will bring us. The name is doubly appropriate because he is being named after Rabbi Meir, the sage who grappled with the deaths of his two sons but remained faithful to God.

But all of our children have second names as well, and Tzvi and I are still not sure what Meir's will be. While we are still in the hospital, he tells me he has found the name. "His middle name," says Tzvi, "should be Emanuel."

"No," I quickly reply. "No names that mention God."

Emanuel means "God is with us," and it is precisely the type of name I wish to avoid. I have remained faithful, but I still haven't forgiven God for all that we have endured. I haven't come to terms with how He abandoned us. No, thank you very much. I will not be reminded of the God who betrayed us every time I call this child's name. How can we honestly say that God is with us?

Tzvi understands how I feel. I've shared this with him before. No names that mention God, I've told him, no Refael, no Daniel, no Michael, nothing.

"Yaffa," he says gently, "can you honestly look into this baby's face and still believe God is not with us?"

And this is when I lower my head and begin to cry, because it's true, and I know it's true. There were thousands of prayers for Dovie's recovery, and he died anyway. But I also prayed for this child. It was one simple, pure request—and I got the answer I wanted. *Give me a healthy child, a child full of goodness, a child filled with love.*

I wipe my tears and nod my head. "Meir Emanuel it shall be," I say.

Our son is born on Shabbat, the 16th of Sivan 5767, just four days after Dov's yahrtzeit. June 2, 2007. I'm disappointed that it's not the same day, until I realize that his *bris* will take place on June 9, the very same day that, just a year before, we buried Dov. And it will take place on Shabbat.

I admit it: I'm impressed by God. The timing is impeccable, and the message is unmistakable. I call my cousin, Esther Nitzlich, to inform her of the birth, and I tell her about when the *bris* is taking place.

"You realize that the *Abishter* is telling you something," she says. "He is saying that it's time to get on with your life."

And so, on Friday, June 8, 2007, exactly one year after we gathered at our house with family and friends to plan a funeral, we convene again at our house to celebrate a birth. My mother-in-law and parents are there, as are my siblings, including Adina, who has arrived with an enormous bouquet of helium balloons. Barbara Price and Judy have helped arrange housing for the thirty-plus guests who will be with us for Shabbat. I remove the four thick binders filled with sympathy cards from our coffee table, and our living room, where we set up for shiva just a year ago, becomes a huge dining room. Among others, we use the four new chairs I bought a few months ago before Yom Kippur. On Friday night, scores of people arrive at our house for the *Shalom Zachar*, and now, instead of offering condolences, they offer congratulations.

After a full year of pain, we experience a palpable, sweet joy unlike any I have ever felt before. The burden has not been removed, but it's noticeably lighter, and the broken family I kept seeing in our pictures now appears, in my mind, to be renewed.

On Saturday, June 9, I dress our infant son, place him in his carriage and, accompanied by family and friends, walk with him across the street to our synagogue. It is the same place and the same time where, one year ago, we gathered for Dov's funeral. Just as it was then, it is packed with people.

Our *mohel* is none other than Rabbi Malka, who had awakened early a year ago to check our mezuzahs. He has told me that it is appropriate for me to say *Birkat Hagomel*, the prayer for thanksgiving, since I have given birth.

I hold the baby, with Sarit at my side. The prayers have ended, and we walk to the men's section to hand my son to Rabbi Malka.

"Now," he whispers.

Allow me to sanctify Your name again by showing the world that You have not forgotten us.

"Blessed are You, Lord our God, King of the universe," I say, "Who rewards the undeserving with goodness, for He has rewarded me with goodness."

Around me, hundreds of people respond: "Amen. May He who has rewarded you with goodness reward you with all goodness forever."

I hand the baby to the *mohel* and, within minutes, our son has been given his name. We are surrounded by family and friends offering mazel tovs. I close my eyes, imagining that Dov is nearby, watching us.

He is smiling, and so am I.

Epilogue

On June 1, 2023, we commemorated Dov's seventeenth yahrtzeit. It was the same day as my son-in-law's birthday. The day before, my cousin's daughter got married, and the day after was Meir's sixteenth birthday. I was struck by how much our lives had changed and grown in the years since we lost Dov; now his yahrtzeit was framed by happy occasions in honor of people who hadn't been part of our lives when he passed away.

In 1996, Dr. Lois Tonkin coined the term "growing around grief" to explain the phenomenon that grief and loss never truly diminish; instead, our lives grow larger around them. After we lost Dov, I learned that life can go on—but only if you allow it to. Moving forward through the pain takes a lot of time, determination, patience, love, and tears. I discovered that, despite the pain that remains with you every day, it is still possible to lead a happy, meaningful life. Undoubtedly, I owe much of that discovery to my wonderful family, friends, and community, who have been with us every step of the way.

In October 2007, we launched dovslist.org and received extremely positive feedback. For several years, it served as an excellent resource for Jewish people experiencing crisis or sickness. However, by 2014, we realized the site was not being used enough to justify keeping it online, and so we made the decision to take it down.

In August 2008, Montgomery County responded to the outcry of our community by implementing a "road diet" to increase safety on Arcola Avenue. The four travel lanes were reduced to two, and "islands" were added in some spots so that there was less road width to cross. As a result of these changes, traffic slowed considerably, and the street became much more pedestrian-friendly. It is truly heartening to know that the accident that killed Dov would be far less likely on the Arcola Avenue of today.

In 2016, we fulfilled our dream of moving to Israel, which is where we live today. That was also the year that our first grandchild was born. He was named after Dov.

We remain in touch with our dear friends in the Kemp Mill Jewish community, who will always hold a special place in our hearts. Every year on Dov's yahrtzeit, Barbara Price sends us a picture of Dov's grave with the many stones that have been placed there in his memory.

We remember him with love.

My brother Yitzie snapped this picture of Dov about a month before his accident.

Tzvi and Dovie, age 1

Hillel, age 1, Dov, age 4, and Sarit, age 3, eating fruit at camp.

One of my favorite photos of Dov as a boy.

Our family at Wheaton Regional Park. L to R, bottom: Hillel, Sarit, Dov, middle: Avichai and Noam. Tzvi and I are on the top.

Tzvi and I posing with Dov at his bar mitzvah.

Dov with his bike in front of our house on Arcola Avenue.

Our family at my brother Akiva's wedding, just nine days before Dov's accident.

Our family in Disney World, October 2006.
We looked happy, but our hearts were broken.

The Sefer Torah dedication in memory of Dov. Tzvi is holding the
Torah we dedicated, and on the right is my father, Rabbi Mordechai
Weiss.

Dov's tombstone.

Our family posing at Noam's wedding in September 2024. R to L, Hillel and his wife Chaya, Avichai and his wife Noam, Tzvi, Noam and his wife Gaalia, me, Meir, Sarit and her husband Tuvia, and their three sons in the front.

Glossary

Abishter – God (Yiddish term)

alav hashalom – May peace be upon him (used after mentioning the name of a deceased person)

aron – Ark (a chest or cabinet in which the Torah scrolls are kept)

Ashkenazic – Relating to Jews of Central and Eastern European descent, as opposed to Sephardic Jews

aufruf – A celebration of a groom being called up to bless the Torah before his wedding

ayin hara – The evil eye, believed to bring harm due to envy or jealousy

bris – Circumcision, a Jewish ritual performed on male infants on the eighth day after birth

chazak chazak v'nitchazek – Phrase said at the completion of reading one of the five books of the Torah, meaning "Be strong, be strong, and we shall be strengthened"

Chazal – An acronym referring to the rabbinic sages of the Talmudic period

chesed – Acts of kindness and giving

chol hamoed – The intermediate days of the Jewish festivals of Passover and Sukkot

chuppah – A canopy under which a Jewish marriage ceremony is performed

daven – To pray (Yiddish term)

Elul – The last month of the Jewish calendar, a time for repentance and self-reflection before Rosh Hashanah

gartel – Yiddish word for "belt," referring to a tie that is placed around the Torah scroll

gut voch – A Yiddish phrase meaning "a good week," typically said following Shabbat

halacha – Jewish law

hamakom yinachem – Phrase said to a mourner who is sitting shiva

hamantash/hamantashen – A three-cornered pastry eaten during the Jewish holiday of Purim, typically filled with poppy seeds or jam

harugai Sho'ah – Victims of the Holocaust

Hashem – God, or literally, "the name." It's a respectful term used to avoid directly naming God

hesped – A eulogy

ilui to their neshamot – Elevation of the souls of the deceased through prayers and good deeds

ir miklat – A city of refuge described in the Torah, designated for people who kill unintentionally

Kaddish – A mourner's prayer recited in memory of a deceased person

kapparos – A Jewish custom of transferring one's sins symbolically by swinging a chicken or money over one's head before Yom Kippur

Kiddush – The blessing sanctifying the Sabbath or Jewish holidays, typically recited over wine or grape juice

Kohanim – Priests, descendants of Aaron, who have specific religious roles in Jewish ceremonies

levaya – A funeral procession

Mah Nishtanah – the four questions recited as part of the Passover Seder

magen – a silver decorative shield that sits on a Torah scroll

mantle – Yiddish word for "coat," referring to a Torah scroll cover

matzeva – A tombstone, typically marking a Jewish grave

mechitza – A partition, used to separate men and women in Orthodox Jewish settings

mezuzah – A parchment scroll with specific Torah verses, placed in a decorative case and affixed to the doorpost of Jewish homes

mikvah – A ritual bath used for purification, such as for conversion or for women after menstruation

minhag – A Jewish custom or tradition

minhag shtut – A custom based on foolishness, referring to a practice that is considered illogical or nonsensical

minyan – A quorum of ten Jewish adults required for certain prayers and religious services

mishebeirach – A prayer for healing, often recited during a Torah reading for those who are ill

mitzvah/mitzvot – A commandment or good deed; mitzvot is the plural form

nisyonos – Tests or challenges

parsha – A weekly Torah portion that is read during Shabbat services

pasul – Unfit for use, typically used in the context of objects that are no longer considered kosher, such as a Torah scroll

Pesach – Passover, a Jewish holiday commemorating the Exodus from Egypt

pesukim – Verses from the Torah or other sacred texts

pikuach nefesh – Saving a life, which can override other commandments

Rambam – Maimonides, a preeminent Jewish philosopher, legal scholar, and physician

refuah – Healing, typically referring to physical or spiritual healing

sefarim – holy books or sacred texts, including the Talmud and prayer books

Sefer Torah/Sifrei Torah – The Torah scroll(s), handwritten on parchment, containing the five books of Moses

segulah – A spiritual remedy or good luck charm, often based on Jewish teachings

Sephardic – Relating to Jews of Spanish, Portuguese, and North African descent

seudat hodaya – A meal of thanksgiving, often following a personal or communal celebration or a miracle

Shabbat – The Jewish Sabbath, observed from Friday evening to Saturday evening as a day of rest

shacharit – The morning prayer service

Shalom Zachar – A celebration held on the Friday night after a boy is born

shavua tov – A Hebrew phrase meaning "a good week," typically said following Shabbat

Shavuot – A Jewish holiday celebrating the giving of the Torah at Mount Sinai

sheva brachot – The seven blessings recited during a Jewish wedding and at subsequent meals

shiur – A lesson or class, often referring to a Torah study session

shiva – The seven days of mourning following a burial

shul – Synagogue, a place of Jewish worship

siddur – A prayer book containing prayers for daily and holiday use

sofer – A scribe trained to write Torah scrolls, tefillin, and mezuzahs.

tallit – A prayer shawl worn during prayers, typically by Jewish men

tashlich – Prayers recited on Rosh Hashanah next to a body of water to symbolize the casting off of sins

tefilla – Prayer

tefillin – Phylacteries, small boxes containing Torah verses, worn by Jewish men during weekday morning prayers

Tehillim – Psalms

teshuva – Repentance, the act of returning to a righteous path after sinning

tevila – Immersion in a mikvah

treif – Unkosher, food that does not meet the dietary laws of Judaism

Tzahal – The Israel Defense Forces

tzedakah – The obligation to give to those in need

yahrtzeit – The anniversary of a person's death, typically commemorated by lighting a candle and reciting Kaddish

yetzer hara – Evil inclination, the part of a person that drives them toward selfishness or wrongdoing

Yizkor – A memorial prayer said for the deceased, typically on major Jewish holidays

Yom Hazikaron – Israel Memorial Day, observed to honor fallen Israeli soldiers and victims of terror

yom tov – Jewish holiday, a day of rest and celebration

Yom Yerushalayim – Jerusalem Day, commemorating the reunification of Jerusalem in the 1967 Six-Day War

Acknowledgements

Writing has always been therapeutic for me, because it helps me organize my thoughts and process my emotions. It was perhaps for this reason that I began keeping a journal in the year after my son Dov passed away. Somehow, putting my feelings on paper allowed me to sort through my grief, and in some small way, to try to make sense of what had happened.

My journal took on a greater role after I was unexpectedly laid off from my job with three months' severance pay and no serious career prospects. That was when I decided to write this book. My son Meir was a baby at the time, and I left him with a sitter while I went to the library to write. I spent many afternoons there, weeping silently in front of a computer screen as I used my journal to write this memoir.

It was the beginning of a project that would take me 18 years to complete, mostly because I kept on stopping and starting again. Each time I worked on this book, I was forced to recall and describe the most painful moments of my life. Many times, I asked myself why I was even bothering. Why not leave the past alone and move forward? Yet I kept on returning to it because I was propelled by what I could only describe as a visceral need to write this story. I had been carrying it with me since I experienced it. I did not know who would read it, but I knew that somehow, I needed to tell it.

I would not have succeeded in doing so without the help and encouragement of many, many people. When my husband Tzvi first read my manuscript, he cried as he turned every page and then told me I needed to publish it. His continuous support and love gave me the fortitude to complete this project.

Along the way, I was fortunate to work with Deborah Meghnagi Bailey, an incredibly skilled and talented editor, who somehow wove my many chapters together into a moving and coherent story. My sister, Adina Ciment, encouraged me every step of the way, even when I despaired of ever finishing. It was she who introduced me to Michael Jenet of Journey Institute Press, who kindly walked me through the very daunting world of book publishing.

I am grateful to the many people who read this book before it was published and offered valuable encouragement, feedback, and advice. My children, Sarit, Hillel, Noam, Avichai, and Meir; my parents, Mordechai and D'vorah Weiss; my siblings, Yitzie, Ari, Akiva, Shimi, and Yoni Weiss, Sarah Cooper, and Elisheva Ben Ze'ev; my aunt, Tova Reich; and my dear friends, Judy Rosenthal and Cindi Dresdner. There were dozens more who read excerpts of the book and generously allowed me to use their names, and I thank them for that.

Finally, I wish to express my deepest thanks and profound gratitude to the entire Greater Washington Jewish community, and to Chai Lifeline and Bikur Cholim of Greater Washington in particular, for all that they did to support and help me and my family when we needed it most. We will never forget their kindness.

Yaffa Klugerman
March 2025

About the author

Yaffa Klugerman is a professional writer and editor, with a background in journalism, public relations, and marketing. Her many articles on Jewish life have appeared in The Forward, The New York Jewish Week, the Washington Jewish Week, the Jewish Telegraphic Agency, and through Behrman House Publishers. She resides in Israel with her husband, children, and grandchildren. *The Broken Vase* is her first book.

About Journey Institute Press

Journey Institute Press is a non-profit publishing house created by authors to flip the publishing model for new authors. Created with intention and purpose to provide the highest quality publishing resources available to authors whose stories might otherwise not be told.

JI Press focusses on women, BIPOC, and LGBTQ+ authors without regard to the genre of their work.

As a Publishing House, our goal is to create a supportive, nurturing, and encouraging environment that puts the author above the publisher in the publishing model.

Storytellers Publishing is an Imprint of Journey Institute Press, a division of 50 in 52 Journey, Inc.